THE
LOST
ZODIAC

The Box of Stars

THE
LOST
ZODIAC

22 ANCIENT
STAR SIGNS

WHAT THEY MEAN AND
THE LEGENDS BEHIND THEM

CATHERINE TENNANT

CHATTO & WINDUS
LONDON

First published 1995

1 3 5 7 9 10 8 6 4 2

Maps by Andras Bereznay

First published in the United Kingdom in 1995 by
Chatto & Windus
Random House, 20 Vauxhall Bridge Road, London SW1V 2SA

Random House Australia (Pty) Limited
20 Alfred Street, Milsons Point, Sydney
New South Wales 2061, Australia

Random House New Zealand Limited
18 Poland Road, Glenfield, Auckland 10, New Zealand

Random House South Africa (Pty) Limited
PO Box 337, Bergvlei, South Africa

Random House UK Limited Reg. No. 954009

A CIP catalogue record for this book
is available from the British Library

ISBN 0 7011 6289 9

Typeset by Deltatype Ltd, Ellesmere Port, Wirral
Printed and bound in China

CONTENTS

~

THE 22 REDISCOVERED STAR SIGNS
The Lost Zodiac

1 PEGASUS
2 ANDROMEDA
3 THE RIVER OF NIGHT (*Eridanus*)
4 PERSEUS
5 ORION
6 THE CHARIOTEER (*Auriga*)
7 THE DOGS (*Canis Major & Canis Minor*)
8 THE SHIP OF THE ARGONAUTS (*Argo Navis*)
9 THE DRAGON (*Draco*)
10 THE GREAT BEAR (*Ursa Major*)
11 THE SEA SERPENT (*Hydra*)
12 THE CUP (*Crater*)
13 THE RAVEN (*Corvus*)
14 THE BEAR KEEPER (*Boötes*)
15 CROWN OF THE NORTH WIND (*Corona Borealis*)
16 THE SERPENT (*Serpens*)
17 THE WISE CENTAUR (*Centaurus*)
18 OPHIUCHUS (*The Serpent Bearer*)
19 THE LYRE OF ORPHEUS (*Lyra*)
20 THE EAGLE (*Aquila*)
21 THE DOLPHIN (*Delphinus*)
22 THE SWAN (*Cygnus*)

STAR DATES

~

DATE	STARS	SIGN
March 13–April 1	Markab	PEGASUS
	Scheat	
	Algenib	
April 2–9	Alpheratz	ANDROMEDA
April 10–18	Acamar	RIVER OF NIGHT
April 19–May 8	Mirach	ANDROMEDA
	Alamach	
May 9–15	Rana	RIVER OF NIGHT
	Zanrak	
May 16–31	Algol	PERSEUS
	Mirfak	
June 1–7	Rigel	ORION
June 8–16	Capella	CHARIOTEER
June 17–27	Betelgeuse	ORION
June 28–July 7	Sirius	DOGS
	Mirzam	
July 8–17	Canopus	SHIP
July 18–25	Procyon	DOGS
	Gomeisa	
July 26–August 7	Gianfar	DRAGON
	Kochab	
August 8–15	Dubhe	GREAT BEAR
	Merak	
August 16–23	Alphard	SEA SERPENT
August 24–	Phekda	GREAT BEAR
September 10	Megrez	
	Alioth	
	Mizar	

DATE	STARS	SIGN
September 11–21	Alkes	CUP
September 22–28	Markeb	SHIP
September 29– October 11	Minkar Algorab	RAVEN
October 12–26	Arcturus Izar	BEAR KEEPER
October 27– November 10	Alphecca	CROWN OF N. WIND
November 11–19	Unuk Elhaia	SERPENT
November 20– December 5	Toliman (Alpha Centauri)	WISE CENTAUR
December 6–16	Han Sabik Ras Alhague	OPHIUCHUS
December 17–23	Grumium Etanin	DRAGON
December 24–28	Alya	SERPENT
December 29– January 13	Vega	LYRE
January 14–28	Altair	EAGLE
January 29– February 8	Rotanev Sualocin	DOLPHIN
February 9–29	Sadir Gienah Deneb	SWAN
March 1–12	Achernar	RIVER OF NIGHT

INTRODUCTION

~

Have you ever read a description of your zodiac sign and thought, 'This isn't really true'? As an astrologer, I too had often looked for reasons to explain traits of character which did not seem to fit with what the zodiac tells us. Perhaps these could be explained by a person's rising sign or moon-sign? It seemed to me that there was something missing. It was my rediscovery of the importance of the stars 'beyond' the zodiac which provided the missing link.

We have grown so used to seeing the traditional zodiac alone as powerful that it comes as a surprise to find that for the early practitioners of astrology, the whole celestial sphere, from pole to pole, was filled with starry gods and supernatural beings who influenced the life of man (and it still is). For them, all the stars had power over our lives. They worshipped them, wove myths around them and built their temples in alignment with them. For the ancient Greeks, therefore, who inherited this vision of a living sphere, and who gave the constellations the names and forms which they still have today, it seemed quite natural to believe that Orion and the Great Bear, Perseus the glittering hero and the Lyre of Orpheus, the legendary musician, among others, influenced our destiny just like the narrow zodiac band of stars which forms the pathway of the sun and moon and planets, with which we are familiar.

The twenty-two 'lost' star signs are the constellations lying to the north and south of the zodiac band, and were used in conjunction with it. They reconnect us to the ancient vision of a sacred, living cosmos, and to the great celestial sphere around us.

The system is similar: as with the zodiac sun signs, all you need to know to find out which constellation rules you is your birthday, not the time of day, the place, or the year. *Unlike* the traditional zodiac signs, whose dates no longer correspond to the positions of the stars in the sky from which they took their names, however, these signs *are* related to the positions of the stars, and *can* be located in the sky. The

~

brightest and most powerful star, or group of stars which fall nearest to the sun, by longitude, on your birthday is 'conjunct' your sun and so rules you. Paradoxically, however, the only time you cannot see your star in the sky is on your birthday, when it is too close to the sun. It is easiest to locate six months from your birthday. The cards and the maps enclosed with the book can be used to discover the shape and position of each constellation, as well as its main stars.

So why did these important star signs, which embody so many of the great myths and symbols of our culture, vanish from the scene? In the second century AD the great astronomer, Ptolemy, pinned our zodiac to the spring and autumn equinoxes, which, together with the zodiac, have gradually moved against the background of the fixed stars. The result has been that the zodiac and the constellations from which each sign took its name, are no longer in alignment and so the influence of the stars, both within the zodiac constellations and beyond them, has been progressively ignored.

When Ptolemy fixed our zodiac to the moving equinoxes, he also tried to simplify astrology by excluding the extra-zodiacal constellations. Even he, however, could not deny their astrological significance, and described the influence of their individual stars. In *L'Astrologie Grecque* (1899), Bouché-Leclerq, the leading authority on the history of astrology, quotes Ptolemy as saying that he will 'leave to one side as impracticable, the ancient method, which took account of all, or nearly all, the stars'. But Bouché-Leclerq continues, 'the exclusion of the constellations beyond the zodiac is so artificial that it could not be maintained, even by Ptolemy . . . all stellar mythology cries out against the privileged position of the zodiac'.

The purpose of this book is not to undermine conventional western astrology, however, which has followed Ptolemy, but to add a lost dimension to it. Valuable as modern astrology may be, it has lost touch with its roots and can no longer be called 'astrology' – the study of the stars – in the strict sense of the word. It concerns itself almost exclusively with the influence of the planets, not of the stars.

These ancient signs are also highly relevant to the times we live in.

Thanks to the moving equinoxes, we are now entering the new Aquarian Age, which is ruled by Uranus, the ancient sky god who personifies the starry sphere and is the ruler of Aquarius. To look beyond our 'seasonal' zodiac, and beyond the 'village' of our solar system, as astronomy is now doing, towards deep space – the domain of Uranus – is, symbolically, in keeping with the spirit of the coming age. One of astrology's most important tenets is that the discovery of a new planet heralds an important change in human consciousness. The discovery of the planet Pluto, in 1930, for instance, which was named after the god of the underworld, and which rules the depths of the unconscious mind, coincided with the rise in popularity of Freud and Jung. The reintroduction of these 'Uranian' signs beyond the zodiac, therefore, and our renewed awareness, when we find our personal star sign in the sky, of our links with the galaxies of stars around us, can be seen to coincide with our entry into the Aquarian age.

From my research as an astrologer, it is remarkable how accurate these rediscovered star signs are. Born under the sign of Andromeda, the princess chained to a rock as a sacrifice for her country, are Houdini, Queen Elizabeth II and Sylvia Pankhurst. I have also found that where the zodiac merely gives us static traits of character, the signs beyond the zodiac are often far richer and more dynamic symbols, as they describe the myths behind our lives and the 'Journey of the Soul of Man': Perseus, of instance, cuts off the gorgon's head and comes to terms with neglected instinct and emotion, which the gorgon represents; the winged horse of inspiration, Pegasus, learns to distinguish between truth and illusion, in the form of the Chimaera; Andromeda, the chained princess, discovers freedom, and the Swan its human form. Ophiuchus wrestles with the Serpent and transforms its poison into medicine; for the great River of Night, which wells up from paradise, life is a journey back towards the sea, where all separate sense of self is lost, and Orpheus overcomes the sovereigns of the underworld with the music of the lyre. Each one has its own personal quest and complements our zodiac signs.

My first real encounter with the signs beyond the zodiac took place about ten years ago, when I read the *Astronomica* of Manilius, the great Roman astrologer and astronomer. Much of the 5th book of the *Astronomica* is dedicated to their meaning, 'the child of the Lyre will sing beguiling songs at the banquet, his voice adding mellowness to the wine and holding the night in thrall . . . and, left to himself, he will ever burst into song which can charm no ears but his own . . . When the Dog Star rises over the rim of the sea . . . it will fashion unbridled spirits and impetuous hearts . . . the child of the Crown [of the North Wind] will cultivate a garden budding with bright flowers, and slopes grey with olives . . . his heart is set upon elegance, fashion, and the art of adornment, upon gracious living and the pleasures of the hour . . .' and so on, at great length, for all the extra-zodiacal signs.

Beautiful as his descriptions are, our understanding of the myths, and of what they can tell us about the soul of man, has changed and grown, of course, since Roman times. What, I wondered, could modern psychology tell us about the meaning of these age-old stories set amongst the stars, and so about ourselves?

With the help of Jungian psychology, which I had studied for many years, and of the modern school of astrology, which uses myth and symbol to give the zodiac and the planets a new, and deeper, meaning, I began to see what it could mean to be born under these 'new' signs. I then applied this to famous people both alive and dead, and to my family and friends. Straightaway the results were startling. As I continued, an image grew and crystallized of the kind of person each one represented, and of the life-issues with which they were most concerned. As with the zodiac, each one had its own preoccupations, its own problems and its own outlook on the world. But the rediscovered signs are different, and I believe that they are more accurate, and more revealing than the zodiac sun signs, because they tell us where our lives are leading and describe our inner quest. The result is a rich new astrological dimension which sheds a much truer light on our characters.

∾

Each star sign from the Lost Zodiac has its own legends, influences and characteristics, as well as its guiding star, its own precious stone and its special plant. All these can be found in the following pages, together with lists of famous people who share the same sign and were born under the same influences.

As the equinoxes gradually move against the backdrop of the fixed stars, by the year 2020 the cusps given in this book will have moved forward by one day. The cusps of the Crown of the North Wind, for example, which now fall on October 27 and November 10, will have changed to October 28 and November 11. In the lists of famous people born under each sign, this shift over past centuries has been taken into account. This means that those born on the same day, even as little as 100 years apart, may not have been born under the same sign. Over a 26,000 year period, therefore, the signs of the 'tropical', or traditional, zodiac, will have been exposed to the influence of the entire range of the Lost Zodiac Signs.

HOW TO USE THE MAPS AND CARDS

∼

To locate your ancient star sign, and your personal guiding star in the night sky, you will need to use the star maps and the cards included.

First, turn to pages viii–ix of the book to discover which star-sign rules you. Then select the card marked with its name. Your guiding star, together with the other important stars in your constellation, is marked on it. Next, read the instructions on the back of the card, to discover in which hemisphere it lies and how to find it.

Now, find it on the map. If you are in the northern hemisphere turn the map until the month when you are using it is at the bottom. The map will then show the sky as it appears while facing south at 10 pm local time (11 pm daylight saving time).

Turn the map clockwise by 15 degrees – half a month marked on the rim – for each hour before 10 pm, and 15 degrees anti-clockwise for each hour after 10 pm.

If you are in the southern hemisphere, the map of the southern hemisphere will show the sky as you face north instead of south. Turn the map in the opposite direction to the instructions for the northern hemisphere.

If your star-sign constellation lies in the southern hemisphere and you are viewing from the northern hemisphere, or vice versa, your constellation will not be marked on the map of the hemisphere you are in. To find it, locate it on the relevant map and follow the instructions on the back of the card.

∼

STAR SIGNS

~

with Legends, Influences
& Characters

PEGASUS
The Winged Horse

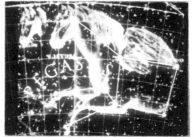

March 13–April 1

GUIDING STARS: The stars of the 'Great Square' of Pegasus, the golden-maned, winged horse of inspiration, lie between Andromeda, the Dolphin and the Swan. Ancient astrologers believed that all the stars of Pegasus protected horsemen in battle.

Those born between *March 13 and 26* are ruled by **Markab** – the blue-white star which marks the horse's shoulder, bringing riches and honour – and the red giant **Scheat**, which marks the horse's leg.

Algenib, which lies at the tip of the horse's outstretched wing, rules those born between *March 27 and April 1*. This star was known in China as one of the 'Three Guides'.

PRECIOUS STONE: Jacinth

PLANT: Moonwort (the fern *Botrychium lunarium*, whose crescent-moon-shaped fronds were believed to unshoe horses)

The Legends

Pegasus, the white winged stallion, with a mane of gold, is the most famous of all legendary horses, in myths or fairy tales. The horse is a symbol of intuition, and of the instincts, the unseen and unconscious forces which carry us through life, but Pegasus, because he can soar up into the skies, stands for instinct transformed, and for inspiration and imagination.

The father of Pegasus was Poseidon, the Greek god of the sea and of storms. Poseidon was the legendary creator of all horses, and to this day, we call white, breaking waves, driven by the wind, 'white horses'. Pegasus's mother was the Gorgon, Medusa, who is best remembered for her hideous gaze, which had the power of turning men to stone.

Once, however, Medusa was a beautiful woman, whom Poseidon desired. As she stood alone, one day, in the temple of Reason, which was sacred to the stern goddess, Athene, Medusa was overwhelmed by the sea-god, as by a tidal wave, and Pegasus, the winged horse of inspiration was conceived. But he was not destined to be born for a long while, for the chaste and war-like goddess was outraged, and cursed the fair Medusa. Her long hair curled and twisted into hissing serpents, her lovely face contorted and grimaced, and she became a terrifying Gorgon, and was banished to the far west of the world.

There she remained until the hero, Perseus (see p. 30), killed her with the help of the magic sword and shield the gods had given him. From her severed neck sprang Pegasus, the golden-maned, and his twin, the curved sword Chrysaor who is the golden sickle of the moon. And so, at last, in death, Medusa gave birth to the noblest of all the sea-god's horses, for Pegasus was winged, unlike the horses of the sea.

Mounted on the back of Pegasus, Perseus flew across the sea. Far below him, he saw the beautiful princess, Andromeda, chained to a rock, and fell in love with her. (For the full story of Perseus and Andromeda, see p. 15 and p. 29.)

When Pegasus was not engaged in playing the role of noble steed to the conquering heroes, as he did for Perseus and later for Bellerophon, he spent his time upon the mountainous slopes of Helicon, and was the favourite of the muses. There, as Ovid tells us in 'the green bowers of the ancient woods, amidst the caves and grottos and the spangled lawns' of fragrant plants, which deprived serpents of their venom, dwelt the nine daughters of the earth and sky, who were the

Muses of poetry and music. They passed their days in dance and song, and, as dark fell, they wrapped themselves in clouds and came down from the mountain. Then, on still nights, their music could sometimes be heard by men, their celestial voices echoing through the darkness.

Because their hoof-marks look like crescent moons, horses in Greece were sacred to the moon, which, as it lights up the darkness of the night, governs the world of imagination, instinct and intuition to which the horse also belongs. The moon was also thought to be the source of all moisture, and it was believed to be the moon-shaped hooves of Pegasus, that, when they struck the flowering earth, had caused the Muses' fountain of poetic inspiration and imagination to start flowing.

The most famous legend about Pegasus is a story of the triumph of true, inspired imagination over fancy and illusion. Bellerophon, Corinth's bravest hero, was set the task of slaying the Chimaera. This monstrous being, whose name we still use to describe deception and delusion, had the body of a goat, the tail of a dragon, and the head of a lion, which belched out sulphur, smoke and flames. Bellerophon asked the goddess of reason, Athene, for help. His prayers were answered in a dream: the grey-eyed goddess handed him a golden bridle with which to tame Pegasus, who would help him to conquer the Chimaera. When Bellerophon awoke, the bridle was by his side. The hero found the winged horse drinking from a sacred fountain, and, throwing the bridle over him, he mounted on his back and soared into the air. They flew from Greece across the seas to southern Turkey, until, below them, the Chimaera, in her mountain cave, appeared. Bellerophon dropped lead into her mouth, which melted in the flames and killed her.

But one day, the proud hero decided to try and ride the winged horse up to heaven. The gods grew angry, and sent a gadfly to sting Pegasus, who shied and threw his rider. Bellerophon fell 'headlong through the fields of air', and, lamed for life, he then wandered, disconsolate, through the world.

Pegasus, meanwhile, continued upwards to the highest heaven. There, he became the bearer of Zeus's divine lightning, and, during storms, the thunder of his hoof-beats, which had set the rhythms of great poetry on the Muses' mountain, could still be heard, high overhead, as he galloped through the sky.

The Star Sign

The moonlit realm of the imagination, of visions, dreams and intutions, is where those born under the sign of the winged stallion, Pegasus, feel most confident and at home. Often, this realm is more real to them than the everyday, material world, and the tendency to day-dream can be strong. Even in the thick of things, they can seem detached and dreamy, and they often have a faraway look in their eyes.

In childhood, they are fond of solitude, even when it is not forced upon them. They have usually had ample time alone to allow the vivid powers of their imagination to develop. Imagination is the greatest of all gifts, but it can be slow to mature. Like Medusa, who was torn between the power of her feelings – which the sea-god represents – and reason, those born under Pegasus have often had to struggle to find the balance between these two sides of their being. Until they manage this, they can swing, uneasily, between being overwhelmed by their emotions, and trying too rigidly to control them. The power of their imagination is born from this conflict, though, and once they have found the middle ground, the richness of their vision can unfold. Even then, it can be hard for them to keep their feet on solid ground.

They can also seem lazy, and unrealistic, to more earthbound, or intellectual signs, especially when they are in an introverted mood. Appearances are deceptive, however. It may look as if they are doing nothing, but they need to dream to renew contact with the well-springs of their being, and recharge the batteries of their inner life. When they bounce back, they become a source of inspiration to the world around them, and no one is more full of enthusiasm – and drive – than they are.

Nothing seems impossible for a Pegasus when on an up-swing. Their energy may come in fits and starts, which is true of most creative people, but when their imagination is captured by a project, things tend to happen fast. Naturally, as the grand master-planners of a scheme, which is how they see their role, they prefer someone else to deal with the boring details. If no one volunteers, however, the project joins the trail of dreams they often leave behind. This does not worry them unduly, though, as the castle in Spain they have been planning, complete with waterfalls and drifts of lilies, is not only built, but has usually been abandoned in their minds, long before the builder's estimate arrives. Still, even during this stage of their lives they are rarely bored, as they are always dreaming up new, and more exciting, schemes.

Sooner or later, however, they tend to grow dissatisfied with their achievements; and, with renewed determination, they teach themselves to harness their imagination, like Bellerophon, using reason and control. Once they have slain the monster of delusion, they are no longer at the mercy of their powerful imagination, and there is little they cannot achieve.

Their relationships with others can also follow the same pattern. They can be fired with enthusiasm for a mysterious face across the room, and even before they meet will have imagined everything about this person – and their future together will be already planned. Being with a Pegasus can be exhilarating and inspiring. But the reality of daily life, of course, can be a different matter, as it is not easy for a mere mortal to live up to their expectations. Once they become bored or disillusioned – when they find out that a real person is quite different from their dream – they will spread their wings and head for new, greener pastures: the hardest thing for Pegasus is learning to accept the limitations of this world.

Once they have learned to exercise control and use reason, their relationships become more earthed and stable. They may still fly off in their imagination, but they become less restless when they discover what a green and pleasant place this earth can be, when it is watered by the refreshing and inspiring wells and springs which they are so gifted at creating. Because of this gift, like Pegasus, who was the favourite of the Muses, they usually have many friends amongst creative people, and the world of art and music is their natural choice for a career and one where they often do well.

But their ability to inspire others is not all that they have to offer. Once they have come to terms with life, and learned to tell the difference between truth and fantasy, between reality, and the Chimaera, their judgement is unequalled. In the end, they can become the greatest realists, and their insight and advice are nearly always razor-sharp.

BORN UNDER PEGASUS: Rudolf Nureyev, Sergei Diaghilev, Vincent Van Gogh, Albert Einstein, René Descartes, Frederik Willem de Klerk, Stéphane Mallarmé, Paul Verlaine, Johann Strauss, Sergei Rachmaninov, Mstislav Rostropovich, Georg Philipp Telemann, Nicholas Rimsky-Korsakov, Sir Richard Burton, Ayrton Senna, Roger Bannister, Bernardo Bertolucci, Marcel Marceau, Stephen Sondheim, William Morris, Andrew Lloyd Webber, Aretha Franklin, Elton John, Gloria Swanson, Steve McQueen, Eric Clapton, Robert Frost, Hans Christian Andersen, St Teresa of Avila.

Pegasus and the Traditional Zodiac

March 13–20   Pegasus and PISCES

Pegasus, the son of the sea-god, gives wings to Piscean creativity and intuition. The horse's drive and inspiration – once bridled – can help Pisces to give form to his dreams, and this is a very dreamy combination.

March 21 – April 1   Pegasus and ARIES
These are the most creative Arians, for Pegasus adds great imagination to the fiery Ram and gives him wings to fly. To get the most out of this dynamic combination, though, it is even more essential that the Winged Horse should be bridled with the help of discipline and reason, as there can be a tendency to fly too fast and high.

Relationships with Other 'Lost Zodiac' signs

Pegasus with THE EAGLE
These are two of the airiest signs and when they get together the earth below almost disappears from sight. The eagle can be annoyed by the horse's tendency to day-dream, though, but when they are in tune, this can be a dazzling combination.

Pegasus with THE LYRE
Both these signs are dreamers and romantics and they often fall in love with one another. Until they learn to be more practical and realistic, though, not much tends to be achieved.

Pegasus with PERSEUS
Perseus is as airy and fast-moving as the winged horse, who is his greatest friend and ally, and they will always help each other as they have a natural understanding.

ANDROMEDA
The Chained Princess

April 2–9 & April 19–May 8

GUIDING STARS: Those born between *April 2 and 9* are ruled by
Alpheratz, or Sirrah, the blue-white star which marks the chained
princess's head, and also forms a corner of the 'Great Square' of
Pegasus, the adjoining constellation. Early astrologers believed that
Alpheratz gave great intelligence, and a desire for freedom, as well as
love and riches, to those born under it.

April 19 – May 8 Those born between these dates have as their stars
Alamach, which marks Andromeda's chained foot, and **Mirach,**
which marks her waist, and which was believed to give great beauty,
intelligence and compassion.

PRECIOUS STONE: Pearl

PLANTS: Bog Rosemary (*Andromeda polifolia*)

The Legends

The stars which cluster around the North Pole have been seen as the
celestial Royal Family since astronomy began, at least 4000 years
ago, on the banks of the great rivers, the Tigris and Euphrates. They
are the rulers of 'the still point in the turning world', and the king,

who sits on his throne, his left foot firmly planted on the Pole, was believed by the Babylonians to be the son of the inventor of astronomy. For the Greeks, however, they were Cepheus and Cassiopeia, the king and queen of Ethiopia, and their daughter, Andromeda, was the princess in the stars nearby.

Cassiopeia was beautiful but she was vain, treacherous and proud. She boasted one day that she was more beautiful than any of the fifty thousand sea-nymphs, and the nymphs were outraged. They turned to the sea-god, Poseidon, demanding revenge, and he in answer, sent a vast female sea-monster to lay waste the kingdom. The Ethiopians, overwhelmed by tidal waves and storms, forced King Cepheus to consult the oracle for help. It told him that the only way to save his land and people was to sacrifice his daughter, Andromeda, to the monster. Straight away, the Ethiopians chained her, naked and decked with sacrificial jewels, to a rock on the sea shore.

But Andromeda was not doomed to die, for the shining hero, Perseus, was at hand to save her. Perseus, who was returning from the Gorgons' lair with Medusa's head, which had the power of turning men to stone, suddenly appeared above her in the clear blue sky, riding on the white winged horse of inspiration, Pegasus. As he looked down, he saw the beautiful princess and fell in love with her. Perseus told the king and queen, who were standing near by, trembling, that he would save their daughter from the monster if he could have her hand in marriage. They hurriedly agreed, and Perseus killed the monster.

Once the monster was dead, however, Cepheus and Cassiopeia changed their mind; but Andromeda, who was in love with Perseus, insisted that the marriage go ahead. During the great wedding feast, the palace doors swung open, and King Cepheus's aged uncle, Agenor, Andromeda's incestuous former suitor, entered at the head of an armed party, to claim his great-niece's hand, followed by Cassiopeia who cried out fiercely that Perseus must die. In the fight that followed, Perseus was outnumbered and was forced to use the

Gorgon's terrifying head against his foes. He raised it up and turned two hundred men to stone.

Poseidon's final revenge on Cassiopeia, for her vanity and for her treachery to Perseus, was to set her image in the stars, where she now hangs, forever upside-down, circling around the North Pole on her throne. Andromeda, however, thanks to her courage and her love, would later gain a far superior place among the stars.

Perseus and Andromeda returned to the land of his birth. There, Perseus accidentally killed his grandfather, and, overcome with grief, exchanged his rightful kingdom for another one near by. They then had many children – one of whom, Gorgophone, was famous as the first widow in legend ever to remarry – and founded a long line of heroes (See Perseus, p. 29.)

The 'Ethiopia' of the story is said to have been a kingdom on the coast of Israel, and the rock to which Andromeda was chained is still shown today near Joppa.

Although Andromeda has become a symbol for the archetypal damsel in distress, waiting for her knight on a white charger, she was once a far less passive and more powerful being. Like Venus, who was born from the foam of the sea, Andromeda, whose name means 'the ruler of men', and who stands naked and bedecked with jewels on the sea shore, is really an ancient love goddess. As Astarte, who was worshipped in temples all along the coast of Israel, she is the goddess of love and the sea.

The whole drama dates back to an earlier era. The sea-monster killed by Perseus was once the Great Goddess, who was the ocean and the source of all life. Only later, when she had been supplanted by the newer sky-gods, was she seen as evil and transformed into a monster, a threatening female figure for men to overcome. Cassiopeia, too, must once have been an image of the Great Mother. While Cepheus, the king, still rules the Pole, Cassiopeia has been humbled, like the goddess who was turned into a monster, and must spin forever round the heavens upside-down, just as her once all-powerful daughter,

Andromeda, is now portrayed in chains. Even so, the story has a happy ending. For Perseus, the heroic stand-in for the sky-gods, loves Andromeda, the goddess, and saves her from the monstrous fate of being devoured and destroyed. And their constellations, which lie side by side amongst the stars, are of equal size and grandeur.

The Star Sign

Those born under Andromeda, the princess in the stars, are loyal and warm-hearted; they are also highly sensitive to the atmosphere around them, and can usually sense other people's feelings – and their motives – from an early age. This can be a mixed blessing for them, as they pick up on not only what is said, but also on all that is *not* said – or done. Every family – and society – of course, has its accepted rules and taboos, without which it could not function. It usually also has its ambitions and pretensions, of which the sensitive Andromedas are often painfully aware. Because they see their loved ones' good points too, however, they try hard to ignore these faults, and so do not at first openly rebel. As a result, like Andromeda, they feel trapped and helpless, especially when they are young – even if their background isn't in fact stifling. In many cases they may feel that, somehow, they are being prevented from being themselves.

But Andromeda, as we have seen, is far more than the passive victim of her past and of convention. For she is 'the ruler of men', the ancient and bejewelled goddess of love and the sea. Those influenced by her are powerful and highly individual people, although at first they may not seem to be so, as it can take time for them to break their chains and find themselves. Because they feel so strongly, it can be hard for them to be objective and to separate their emotional loyalties from their beliefs. Once they have learned to discriminate and to think more clearly, instead of simply reacting and protesting, they can discard those values which they do not like and choose their own course. And, having realized that other people are just as much the victims of circumstance as they are, or were, themselves, they can set about the work of liberating others.

Freedom, both for herself and others, is Andromeda's true goal in life; from Marx and Freud to Oliver Cromwell and Houdini, those born under the princess in the stars are chain-breakers, many of whom have been responsible for the most important changes in the way we think and live our lives.

Before they learn self-knowledge, however, they can be unduly self-pitying. They complain about their problems to friends and lovers, expecting others to play the knight in shining armour to their damsel in distress. They can also be high-handed – they are princesses after all – expecting others to drop everything to help them, whenever they're called. They often get their own way, however, as they usually have great charm – and style. Even when they are complaining, their real self – of which the powerful ancient goddess is a symbol – can be seen, glinting through, from beneath the surface.

Not everyone can be Perseus (see p. 29), the mercurial, airborne hero, who is Andromeda's soul-mate, and who frees her from her chains, but there are usually plenty of people who would happily step in and play the role. Only when the real Perseus comes along, is she saved because he knows, at first hand, what she is going through. For when Perseus meets Andromeda, he has already slain the Gorgon, the monstrous being whose gaze turns men to stone, and who represents for him the same repressed instincts and emotions as the sea-monster who threatens to devour Andromeda. Perseus is the great innovator, who sees life from a new angle, the high-flying, fast-moving thinker who can take a bird's eye view, breaking with the habits of the past and offering a fresh solution, which is what Andromeda most needs and longs for. Andromeda, in turn, can offer him a normal life – once she herself is free – and bring him down to earth, so that concrete, lasting and creative changes can be made.

But Andromeda can free herself without a prince on a white

charger. All that is required, as we have already seen, is for her to become detached, if only for a while, from her emotions, and take a 'Perseus'-eye view' of herself, and of her world, with its values and assumptions. And, strangely enough, it is usually then, and only then, that a real-life Perseus makes his entrance on the scene.

Once those born under Andromeda are free, they nearly always dedicate their time and energy to trying to improve the lot of others. While Perseus's realm is action and abstract thinking, those influenced by Andromeda are, above all, the champions of the oppressed and the down-trodden. And, like Sylvia Pankhurst, who chained herself to the railings to win the vote for women, they are often prepared to sacrifice their hard-won freedom to help others.

BORN UNDER ANDROMEDA:Lenin (Vladimir Ilyich Ulyanov), Maximilien Robespierre, Sigmund Freud, Ludwig Wittgenstein, Karl Marx, Oliver Cromwell, John Brown, Sylvia Pankhurst, Maia Angelou, Mary Wollstonecraft Godwin, Nellie Bly, Dr Spock, Max Ernst, Max Planck, Guglielmo Marconi, Charles Baudelaire, Billie Holliday, Ella Fitzgerald, Elizabeth II, Emperor Hirohito, Golda Meir, Robert Oppenheimer, Marshal Tito, Harry Houdini.

Andromeda and the Traditional Zodiac

April 2–9, April 19–20   Andromeda and ARIES
The fiery, pioneering sign of Aries gives Andromeda the energy and drive to break her chains and free herself and others, while the influence of Andromeda makes these Arians both more compassionate and more down to earth.

April 21 – May 8   Andromeda and TAURUS
On the plus side, this combination gives great staying-power and strength, but it can be harder for them than it is for those born under Aries to see things from a new perspective.

Relationships with Other 'Lost Zodiac' Signs

Andromeda with PERSEUS
Obviously, this is the ideal combination, as the story shows . . .

Andromeda with ORION
The golden huntsman, Orion, is also a good partner for Andromeda. Orion has no time for social rules and restrictions, and so can sympathize with the chained princess. She, in turn, can help him to understand how other people think, and is grateful for the freedom which she gets with him.

Andromeda with CROWN OF THE NORTH WIND
Those born under Andromeda have a lot in common with those ruled by the Crown of Ariadne and her labyrinth. Both are trapped by their culture and conditioning, but Ariadne has the thread to find the path to freedom which Andromeda needs.

THE RIVER OF NIGHT
Eridanus

March 1–12, April 10–18 & May 9–15

GUIDING STARS: *April 10–18* These dates are ruled by **Acamar**, which for the ancients in the northern hemisphere, who were unable to see Achernar in the south, marked the end of the River and was the River's most important star.

Zanrak, the Bright Star of the Boat, rules *May 9–15*. It lies not far distant from Orion, and can be seen more easily from northern latitudes. It is said that those born under its influence should try to take life less seriously, and should not pay too much attention to the opinions of others.

Those born between *March 1 and 12* are guided by **Achernar**, the End of the River. This blue giant is the ninth brightest star in the heavens and is supposed to have been mentioned by Dante, although it is invisible from Italy, and is best seen from the southern hemisphere. It is a thoughtful, philosophical and optimistic star.

PRECIOUS STONE: Amber

PLANT: Poplar

The Legends

Life and Time, flowing from an unknown source, were envisaged in the ancient world as a great river, welling up from the beyond.

The River Eridanus, whose heavenly counterpart, the River of Night (as it was called in Babylon), flows down from the stars around Orion's feet towards the Southern Pole, was thought by the Greeks to come from paradise, the timeless Islands of the Blessed. The story of the Eridanus is also the story of the proud and foolish Phaethon, Helios the sun-god's handsome son, who pleaded with his father to be allowed to drive his blazing chariot for one day. With the inexperienced hands of Phaethon on the reins, the Sun's bright horses bolted through the heavens, scorching the earth and drying up the rivers. North Africa was turned into the Sahara, and to save the universe, which would have been destroyed by flames, Zeus struck Phaethon with a thunderbolt, and he plunged headlong, like a shooting star, into the waters of the Eridanus far below, his auburn hair aflame. His sisters, the Heliades, who came to mourn for him, were transformed into poplar trees, and their tears turned into drops of amber, the river's jewel, which was found along its banks. His friend and lover, Cycnus, also came to weep for him and was transformed into a swan.

The heavenly river is also Oceanus, the ancients' Ocean Stream, which encircled the whole universe. From it arose all the stars – with the exception of the Great Bear – only to plunge back again, like Phaethon. Married to his sister Tethys, with whom he shared a palace in the far west of the world, Oceanus was the essence of all things. He was the father not only of three thousand rivers and of three thousand sea-nymphs, but of the sea and of all the waters which gushed forth from the earth as springs.

To the ancient Greeks, all the streams and rivers were alive. The rivers, depicted as vigorous young men with horns and beards, were worshipped by the young, who sacrificed their hair to them. Oaths were sworn in their name, and horses, bulls and rams were thrown into their waters as offerings to the gods who dwelt in them. The

with whoever cares to listen. Like the water-nymphs, those ruled by the River also have an insight into situations and character that can verge on the prophetic, as their intuition hardly ever lets them down.

In many ways those born under this sign are wanderers and loners, but, as we have already seen, their destination is the ocean and their deepest instinct is to unite with others – preferably, the whole world, but failing that, with others of like mind. Until they run into someone who can really share their goals, they can be lonely. When they find true kindred spirits, they stick by them to the end, and are always happy to share whatever comes; provided, of course, that the other person does not try to slow them down or trap them, and as long as they share a common goal.

They may not like feeling trapped or stagnant but they do enjoy tranquillity, and when they are content in their relationships, they are great life-givers and enhancers. Without the River's fertilizing waters, this world would be a desert; River people can create an atmosphere of peace and gentleness, of green and tranquil meadows, which is almost unrivalled.

But their desire to merge with others on equal terms is only one aspect of the River's complex emotional nature. They can also use their charms for better or worse. They can be helpful and inspiring, but they can also be destructive and deceptive, lulling others into wasting time with them and like the water-nymphs, luring them away from the real world – although they would react violently if anyone tried to do the same to them.

The River has another unique gift. Water is nature's only mirror, and people involved with those born under this sign can find it hard to get to know them, as they can, and do, reflect whatever face is shown to them. One can learn a lot about oneself, which can be an education, but very little about them, unless they choose to let you see beneath their often sparkling and mysterious surface. Their reluctance to show their true feelings is often a defence, as the River is one of the most emotional and sensitive of signs.

As they mature, however, those born under the sign of the River move beyond their wild, tempestuous phase, and it is often in the second half of life that they really come into their own. Then, with mountains and steep ravines behind them, they can meander through the plains and open valleys, their powerful feelings changed by time to wisdom, and they often grow into the great philosophers – and civilizers – of mankind. Thanks to their sense of harmony and flow, they are also often singers, poets, or musicians.

BORN UNDER THE RIVER OF NIGHT: Maurice Ravel, Antonio Vivaldi, Glenn Miller, Fred Astaire, Hector Berlioz, Kiri Te Kanawa, Kurt Weill, Harry Belafonte, Florence Nightingale, Dante Gabriel Rossetti, Mikhail Gorbachev, Michelangelo, James Dean, J. M. Barrie, Thornton Wilder, Henry James, Kenneth Grahame, Daphne du Maurier.

The River and the Traditional Zodiac

April 10–18   The River and ARIES
As Aries is a fiery and impetuous sign, those born beneath this combination are more passionate and moody than those influenced by River–Pisces. They also reach their destination a lot faster, and, strangely, are far less stubborn than their Piscean cousins.

May 9–15   The River and TAURUS
This is the calmest and the least tempestuous and moody combination. Still waters run deep for River–Taurus, which is also the most able to create an atmosphere of peace and harmony. It is, however, the most stubborn combination.

March 1–12   The River and PISCES
These two water signs have a lot in common, and those born under them appear more passive and easygoing than those Rivers influenced by fiery Aries. They are, in fact, just as determined, although

Perseus and his mother lived, banished after his birth), who wished to marry Danaë against her will, sent Perseus to bring back the head of the Medusa, an appalling Gorgon with serpents in her hair, whose petrifying gaze turned all who looked her in the face to stone. The king imagined that he was sending Perseus to his death, but fate was on the hero's side. So were the gods.

Athene, the grey-eyed goddess of reason and reflection, gave him her burnished shield, a highly polished mirror, so he could use its reflective surface to help him see to cut off the Gorgon's head without being turned to stone. Even Hades, the dark lord of the Underworld and death, helped him in his battle against evil, lending him the helmet which made anyone who wore it vanish, like the dead, from view. Hermes, the messenger of the gods, gave him a curved dagger made of diamonds, and his winged sandals, in which Perseus soared up, unafraid, into the blue Aegean skies. Like his constellation, which travels westwards through the heavens every autumn, Perseus journeyed through the air towards the Gorgons' lair in the far west of the world.

As he approached the lonely dwelling, he put on the helmet of invisibility and raised the mirrored shield. In it, he saw reflected three archaic and barbaric beings lying asleep, with their brass hands, boar's teeth and serpent hair. They were surrounded by the surreal, rain-worn shapes of men and animals, whom their gaze had turned to stone. Perseus raised his diamond sword and struck off Medusa's head. From her severed neck sprang Pegasus, the white, winged horse of inspiration, and his twin, Chrysaor, her hitherto unborn children.

Perseus thrust the awful head into a magic wallet he had brought with him, and fled from the remaining gorgons, this time on the back of Pegasus, airborne, like the stars named after him, once again.

As he flew, drops of blood fell from Medusa's head into the sea, and created the first coral. Suddenly, far below, he saw Andromeda, chained, naked, to a rock and hung with jewels, about to be devoured by a sea-monster. Perseus fell instantly in love with her, and, swooping down, he killed the great sea-monster with his diamond sword.

As soon as Perseus and Andromeda were married, they returned to Seriphos, arriving just in time to prevent the rape of Perseus's mother, Danae, by the king, who was turned to stone, together with all his courtiers, by Medusa's head.

Perseus then returned the magic shield, sword and sandals, and gave the Gorgon's head to Athene, who placed it on her shield, a symbol of reason's triumph over instinct and barbaric evil.

They then set off for the land of Perseus's birth, where the hero, joining in the local games, threw a quoit which accidentally killed his grandfather, as the oracle had foreseen. Perseus was heartbroken, and, to put the past behind him, he exchanged his rightful kingdom for another. There, Perseus and Andromeda had many children, and founded a long line of heroes. They also founded the legend-haunted citadel of Mycenae, where what must be the Gorgon's flower, the sinister snake's-head fritillary, now grows wild amongst the ruins.

The Star Sign

Perseus, the 'shining one', is the airiest and brightest of the heroes, and those born under the symbol of this Clark Kent of the ancient world are fast-moving, witty and mercurial, with an edge and sparkle which ensures that they are never dull or heavy-handed. Interested in anything and everything, they will pursue whatever fires their imagination with great energy and drive, until they tire of it, which can happen with alarming speed when something new and more exciting comes along. Which it usually does, as they are always on the look-out for amusement and distraction. Without novelty, in fact, or mental stimulation, they become not only restless but depressed, and there is no sadder sight than a Perseus tied to a life of drudgery and routine.

Not that they often are, though, as they can talk themselves out of almost any corner, and they usually find someone who will believe in their new schemes, and is prepared to help them out. They often get

Perseus and the Traditional Zodiac

May 16–20   Perseus and TAURUS

Perseus adds speed and sparkle to the earth-bound sign of Taurus, while Taurus acts as a steadying ballast to the glittering hero. This is a balanced combination, although it can lack the brilliance of Perseus–Gemini.

May 21–31   Perseus and GEMINI

These are the most quick-witted and mercurial Geminis of all, as Perseus is very similar to Hermes, the airborne messenger of the gods, who lent Perseus his winged sandals, and who, as Mercury, rules Gemini.

Relationships with Other 'Lost Zodiac' Signs

Perseus with ANDROMEDA

This is a great love-match, as the story tells us, as Perseus can help the chained princess to find her freedom, and she, in turn, can help him to learn to live on earth.

Perseus with PEGASUS

These high-flying allies always get on well, although they share a tendency to avoid responsibility.

Perseus with the DRAGON

These signs have a lot to offer one another. The Dragon needs to transform its instincts and emotions into vision, which Perseus can help it to achieve. The Dragon, in turn, can help Perseus to face up to his instinctual side, instead of flying off into the airy abstract realm.

Perseus with THE EAGLE

Perseus and the Eagle have a lot in common, and the Eagle's great determination can help Perseus to achieve his aims.

ORION
The Hunter

June 1–7 & June 17–27

GUIDING STARS: **Rigel**, the Mariners' Star, a blue-white supergiant 57,000 times brighter than our sun, rules the dates *June 1–7*. Early astronomers believed that it conferred splendour and honours upon those born under its influence.

June 17–27 are governed by **Betelgeuse**, a giant, red-topaz-coloured star, which rises in the autumn just as Antares, the red star heart of the Scorpion which killed Orion, sets. A warlike star, Betelgeuse was believed to bring courage, wealth and honour.

PRECIOUS STONES: Emerald and Opal. Orion was worshipped in ancient Babylon as the god who created precious stones.

PLANT: Martagon Lily (*Lilium martagon*)

The Legends

Orion was a giant so tall that he could wade through the deepest ocean with his head above the water. His strength and beauty were legendary, as was his love of hunting, and, like his stars, which wander endlessly across the heavens, he was destined for adventure.

After his first wife was banished to the Underworld for boasting

solitary part of him which remains both innocent and untamed. This is the aspect of Orion which belongs to Artemis, the virgin huntress, goddess of the crescent moon. Without it and without the contact with nature, pure and simple, which she represents, he would lose his strength and innocence, and his way in life.

BORN UNDER ORION: Jean-Jacques Rousseau, Paul Gauguin, Robert Falcon Scott (of the Antarctic), Bjorn Borg, Johnny Weissmuller ('Tarzan'), Juan Fangio, Jack Dempsey, Marilyn Monroe, George Bryan 'Beau' Brummell, Isabella Rossellini, Jane Russell, H. Rider Haggard, Errol Flynn, Thomas Hardy, Helen Keller, St John of the Cross, Empress Josephine, Pearl S. Buck, Edward Elgar (composer of the *Enigma Variations* of which one was 'Nimrod' the Great Hunter), King Henry VIII, George Mallory (the mountaineer), King George III, King George V, Nicolas Poussin (who painted Orion).

Orion and the Traditional Zodiac

June 1–7, June 17–21   Orion and GEMINI
Although Gemini is an intellectual air sign, it has a lot in common with Orion. Geminis are forever trying to find a way to make peace between the two sides of their being. Like Orion, they see the world too much in terms of black and white, and the story of Orion's blinding, and how he finds wisdom and compassion through experience, shows the way for Geminis to overcome the split within themselves and find a balance.

June 22–27   Orion and CANCER
Ruled by the moon, Cancer expresses Orion's link with Artemis and nature in its purest form.

Relationships with Other 'Lost Zodiac' Signs

Orion with THE GREAT BEAR
The Great Bear is a symbol of the moon goddess and those born under it can play the role of Artemis in Orion's life.

Orion with THE BEAR KEEPER

The Bear Keeper is the son of the Great Bear, and so of Artemis, and its natives have much common ground with Orion, sharing his love of adventure and the wilder side of life.

Orion with THE DOGS

These are the dogs which follow at Orion's heels and their relationship is self-explanatory: they are his loyal companions and true friends.

Orion with THE RIVER OF NIGHT

The River wells up from Paradise at Orion's feet, and its natives can bring out a more inward-looking and contemplative side of Orion's nature.

THE CHARIOTEER
Auriga

June 8–16

GUIDING STAR: Those born between *June 8 and 16* are influenced by **Capella,** the Goat Star of ancient Babylon. The sixth brightest star in the heavens, it was believed by early astrologers to bring wealth, honour and a position of public trust, as well as a love of knowledge and of novelties.

PRECIOUS STONE: Sapphire

PLANTS: Mint and Mandrake

The Legends

Auriga, the heavenly Charioteer, was believed by the Greeks to have been Erichthonius, the inventor of the horse-drawn chariot, who was immortalized amongst the stars. The child of the god, Hephestus, the lame smith of Olympus, and of Mother Earth, who rejected him at birth, Erichthonius was adopted by the grey-eyed goddess of reason, Athene, who gave him to three Athenian maidens to look after. Athene placed the child in a basket, forbidding them to raise the lid and look inside, but their curiosity got the better of them – when they saw that their charge had a serpent's body, they screamed in terror and jumped to their death off the Acropolis in Athens. Athene then took up the child and placed him in her aegis, a goatskin shield, upon which she carried the severed head of the snake-haired Medusa, whose gaze had once turned all who looked on her to stone. Although Athene was a virgin goddess and had no children of her own, she tended Erichthonius with such loving care that he looked upon her as his mother. She also gave him two phials of Medusa's blood, which she tied to his serpent-body with bands of gold. The blood in one phial, which had been drawn from the left side of the Gorgon's body, was lethal to anyone who came in contact with it. The blood in the other, however, which came from her right side, had the power to raise the dead. When he grew up, Erichthonius invented the horse-drawn chariot and became the fourth king of Athens, where he introduced the use of silver. He reigned there for fifty years and died, it is said, in 1437 BC.

It was really Athene, however, who was thought to have been the real 'inventor' of the chariot, and, in many ways, as her 'child', Erichthonius is merely an extension of her. To understand exactly who he is, and what he stands for, it is necessary, therefore, to understand the nature of Athene, the goddess of reason and wisdom. She is the patron of all cities, and of civilization in general, who gave the olive tree to Athens, where her worship was established, and which is named after her. She was credited as the inventor not only of the chariot, but of the horse's bridle, the ox-yoke, the ship, the earthenware pot, the trumpet and the flute. She was also said to be the originator of spinning, weaving, cooking and mathematics; and she was, in addition, a goddess of war. Her mercy to mankind, however, was great and she preferred to settle quarrels rather than create them. When she was forced to fight, though, she was unbeatable, as she was an expert in tactics and in strategy of every kind.

Although her goatskin shield adorned with snakes, echoed in Erichthonius's serpent body, relates her to the Mother Goddess of far earlier times, Athene, who had sprung fully-armed from her father,

Zeus's forehead, represents a new relation to the instincts, which the horse she bridled symbolizes. To Perseus, for instance, she lent her mirrored shield, so that he could cut off Medusa's head by taking aim at the reflection, and so avoid being turned to stone by looking directly at her face. She stands, therefore, for the ability to *reflect*, and so for self-discipline, self-mastery, strategy and foresight, which all require consideration and control, and which are qualities that, until Greek times, were not well-developed.

That Erichthonius spent his early days in Athene's goatskin shield, upon which she bore Medusa's head as a trophy of the victory of wisdom and reason over uncontrolled passions and instincts, tells us almost all that we can know about this mysterious king of Athens. With him in the stars are a she-goat and her kids, perhaps a memory of the goatskin shield in which he was brought up. Capella, the Goat Star – the guiding star of those born beneath this constellation – lies in the goat, and not the Charioteer who holds it. This underlines once more, perhaps, the importance of Athene's fostering of this serpent king.

The goat, however, was also thought of as Amalthea, the she-goat who suckled the infant Zeus in a Cretan mountain cave and whose horn was later to become the legendary Horn of Plenty, which gave unfailing nourishment and goodness to mankind.

The Star Sign

This is the most civilized – and civilizing – of the 'Lost Zodiac' signs. Like Athene, the grey-eyed and level-headed goddess who brought up the starry charioteer to govern Athens for her, those born under this sign never move before considering the outcome of their actions, or before they have examined the situation from all sides. They are reasonable and measured in their dealings with the world, and, thanks to their logic, their clarity of thought and their concern for justice, they are also often to be found playing the role of arbitrator in other people's battles. Like Solomon, they can be relied upon to give a fair and balanced judgement, however complex or tangled the problem posed may be, for they are open-minded and scrupulously just.

They are also practical and industrious people who like to use their energy to make real improvements in the world around them, and they consider abstract thought for its own sake – let alone just sitting around dreaming – as both boring and a waste of time. As a result, they are nearly always on the go, whether they are master-minding some new scheme to make the world a better place, or just tidying up or mowing the lawn. They are also the best organizers and planners, holding the reins, like Erichthonius, in their capable, efficient hands, but they are inventive and creative as well, like Athene, the inventor of the chariot, the ship and loom. They are at their happiest, and most relaxed, in fact, when they are following in her footsteps and creating something which is both pleasing to the eye and useful, which makes them feel fulfilled and worthwhile.

However much they contribute to the basic quality of life for others, they can, at times, take their love of Athene's qualities of order and self-discipline just a bit too far and have to pay a price for such control. Because they always try to listen to their head and not their heart, they can become afraid to act on their true feelings – that is, if they still know what they are, as they tend to dismiss as irrational and silly emotions that do not fit with their vision of themselves, in an attempt to keep their lives in order. They can also be too proud to let on how they are feeling, and, as someone once said, where pride is insistent, memory gives way, which means they can find it only too easy and convenient to forget the things that do not suit them – which can be a real problem for the Charioteer.

Feelings which are kept under control, as everybody knows, do not just go away, and, beneath their cool exterior, those born under the Charioteer can feel confused and insecure. Their determination not to pay heed to their emotions, let alone to show them, can be hard to handle for those involved with them, as it makes it difficult to gauge their true reactions or to really get to know them. But, despite their tendency to be distant and aloof at times, they are kind, affectionate people, and, once you win their trust, they will stick by you to the end. The reason for their insecurity is that, like Erichthonius, who never knew his real mother and transferred his loyalty to Athene, queen of reason, they have often been let down at some point in their lives, and it can take time for them to learn to be more trusting. Until they do, everything which is not planned and kept under control – preferably by them – can seem threatening to them. Usually, however, they begin to see, with their well-developed reason, that many of their fears are groundless, and then their outlook becomes a great deal more spontaneous, and they can give their energy and their instinctive side much freer rein.

Once they have found the balance between instinct and reason, chaos and control, they are also far more able not only to relate to others, but to use their creative, civilizing powers in a wide variety of ways. Of all the signs, in fact, the Charioteer is probably the most versatile, and those born beneath it are usually all-rounders who are just as good at sewing as they are at politics, or carpentry, or sport. And, as they are also influenced by the Goat Star's Horn of Plenty, whether they are doctors, judges, jockeys or town-planners, their broad vision, their detachment and their social conscience mean that they are nearly always generous in a practical and caring way to others.

BORN UNDER THE CHARIOTEER: Peter the Great, Anthony Eden, George Bush, Che Guevara, Enoch Powell, Viscount Castlereagh, Kind Edward I, King James I, Admiral Sir Henry Keppel, Peter Scudamore, Giacomo Agostini, John Rennie, Frank Lloyd Wright, George Stephenson, Prince Philip, Thomas Arnold.

The Charioteer and the Traditional Zodiac

June 8–16   The Charioteer and GEMINI

The influence of Gemini gives the Charioteer his speed and airy clarity of thought, while the organizing powers of Auriga give drive and the ability to follow something through. These Geminis, therefore, are the most consistent and the highest achievers amongst those born beneath this changeable, mercurial sign.

The Charioteer and the Other 'Lost Zodiac' Signs

The Charioteer with PEGASUS

Both these signs are concerned with finding the right balance between instinct and reason, but to different ends. Pegasus, the winged horse, is, perhaps, the most imaginative of all the signs, but can need earthing, with which those born beneath the Charioteer can help them. Pegasus, meanwhile, brings out the Charioteer's creative and inventive side and helps him to live more freely.

The Charioteer with THE BEAR KEEPER

These two signs have the greatest powers of organization – and the strongest social conscience. When they operate in tandem, they can move mountains, but they can get on each other's nerves as well, as they both want to hold the reins.

The Charioteer with PERSEUS

Perseus is another sign which is searching for the balance between the rational and irrational sides of life. Perseus, however, lacks the Charioteer's practical approach, which he could well do with more of, while Auriga is, in turn, inspired by Perseus's ability to see a situation from a fresh angle.

The Charioteer with THE RAVEN

The Raven's well-developed powers of intuition make it sympathetic to the problems of the intellectual Charioteer. The Charioteer, in turn, helps the Raven to use its reason and become more balanced.

This is a very good combination, when they learn to understand each other.

Note: Those born between these dates are also influenced by Orion's stars (see page 35), although not so strongly as they are by the Charioteer's.

THE DOGS
Canis Major & Canis Minor

June 28–July 7 & July 18–25

GUIDING STARS: *June 28–July 7* Those born between these dates are ruled by **Sirius**, the Dog Star, which is the main star in Canis Major, the Great Dog. Sirius, the 'sparkling' or the 'scorching', is the brightest star in the heavens, and was thought to cause the stifling heat of the 'Dog Days', which run from July 3 to August 11.

July 18–25 are governed by **Procyon**, the bright star in the Little Dog, Canis Minor.

Both stars were thought by the ancients to inspire a faithful and devoted nature in those born beneath their influence. While the two dogs both pursue the Golden Huntsman, Orion, across the winter skies, the Little Dog was thought by some to be the favourite of Helen of Troy, transferred to the stars.

PRECIOUS STONE: Beryl and Agate

PLANT: Marigold and Mugwort

The Legends

Dogs, in the world of myth, have always been connected with the night and with the goddess of the dark phase of the moon. From the earliest times, they have been seen as the guardians of the mysteries, standing, alert, on the threshold of death and the unknown.

It may seem strange that the faithful and familiar Friend of Man should be linked with the darkness of the other world, but the belief dates from a time when death, like the dark phase of the moon, was seen as part of a great cycle. Like the moon, which waxes, wanes and vanishes before it reappears, it was believed that when we die we are reborn. Death, and the dark phase of the moon, then, were merely the unknown, through which the Dog, with its superior instincts and its ability to follow a scent blindly, was the ideal guide.

The dog, of course, which appears to sense the spirit world around us, also represents our own instinctive side, which can guide us through the unknown regions of the soul.

As time went on, the old religion was replaced by the worship of the sun-gods. Unlike the moon, the sun was always bright and its enemy was darkness. The more brightly shone the sun, and the light of reason, the darker seemed the realm of instinct and the night, and so the underworld became a source of fear and dread, and the dogs, the helpful instincts which had once been our guides, were now seen as a threatening pack of hounds, baying at the moon.

In Greece, dogs belonged to Hecate, the Underworld Queen of the Night, the goddess of witches and of cross-roads – where, ever since, witches have been buried. Before that, however, when the darkness was not feared, Hecate had been seen as 'tender-hearted', for she was really only the goddess of the unknown and of the dark phase of the moon. She carried two torches, the 'brilliant eyes of the dark', which possibly symbolized her power to see things which were hidden from the eyes of others. And, as guardian of the cross-roads, she watched over those moments of uncertainty in life when the future is unknown and undecided. Always, the dogs are by her side. But dogs were also sacred to Artemis, the virgin goddess of hunting and the crescent moon, for dogs, of course, are also hunters.

The dog appears in Egyptian myth as Anubis, the mysterious, dog-headed god who guided the souls of the dead to their judgement. Because the dog is not easily deceived and can sense someone's true nature, it was Anubis's job to weigh the dead man's soul, which was balanced in the scales against the 'feather of truth'.

No one knows why, or when, Sirius became the Dog Star, and was associated with the goddess of resurrection and the dark phase of the moon. Perhaps it was because, on moonless nights, men used the star as a guide, as it is our brightest. Certainly, the links between the goddess and the brightest winter star are very old. So old, in fact, that they have almost been forgotten – but they are there, hidden in the stories.

More than 4,000 years ago in Crete, for instance, dogs were sacred to the bee goddess, whose festival of resurrection, the ancient Cretan New Year, was celebrated when the Dog Star was closest to the sun. (Bees, incidentally, were believed to be the resurrected souls of the dead, and to this day it's thought unlucky not to tell a swarm of bees when their owner dies.)

And in Egypt, the Dog Star is Isis, the great goddess, who, with the help of the dog-headed Anubis, resurrected her husband, Osiris, from the dead. Later, the famous mysteries of Eleusis, in which Demeter, the Greek goddess of the corn, revealed the hidden truth of the soul's rebirth, were held, in darkness, when the Dog Star was at its height.

The Star Sign

Those born under Sirius and Procyon, the bright Dog Stars which follow at Orion's heels, are most at home in the domain of instinct and intuition. Like the Egyptian Anubis, who weighed men's souls, they have almost X-ray vision when it comes to understanding people's motives and emotions, which they sense however well hidden these are. This is because they are always on the look-out for clues. They can glean more from someone's body language, and from what is unspoken – except for the unintentional slips – than most signs ever learn from what is actually said.

As it is so difficult to fool them, they are not easily impressed by glamour and affectation, and they always choose their friends for their true characters, rather than for the face they show the world. Loyalty is the quality, of course, for which the dog is famous, and, true to type, when they do befriend someone, they rarely change their minds or let them down. Nor are they critical, even of those with whom they do not have close bonds, being generous and warm-hearted. They are extremely protective of their loved ones, however, and, if necessary, will risk life and limb to defend them.

Trying to discover other people's motives is only one way in which their boundless curiosity manifests itself. They are fascinated by anything mysterious, occult or unknown, and, like Jung, or the archaeologist, Sir Arthur Evans, who unearthed the legendary Cretan labyrinth, they like to delve beneath life's surface and discover what is hidden. Once they are on the trail of something or someone, they rarely give up the quest until they find what they are looking for, however long it takes, as they are single-minded and determined when their interest is aroused. This tendency can become obsessional at times – a trait which those born under the Dog Stars need to guard against if they are to keep their balance. Putting problems on ice, and allowing situations to change and develop of their own accord, does not come easily to them. They can drive themselves – and those around them – almost crazy, as they find it so hard to sit back and let things be.

These qualities, however, make them the best detectives and explorers. But, like all sleuths, once they have found what they set out for, they lose interest and move on. Even so, they still hang onto their souvenirs, and their homes are often full of trophies from previous chases, gathering dust, as although they are adventurous, they are also sentimental and nostalgic for their past.

Being so curious about the new, and yet so profoundly loyal to their past, can be a tricky combination, and they are happiest in relationships which make room for both aspects of their nature. Ideally, they like to come and go, and the more freedom they are given to pursue their current interests, wherever these may take them, the more certain are they to return.

Those born under the Dogs are gregarious, and, given half a chance, will avoid spending too much time alone. Despite their tendency to be one-track-minded when the mood is on them, in relationships with others they are adaptable and fair. And as they are so warm-hearted, they do not find it easy to hold grudges. Being so perceptive – and sophisticated – about the quirks of human nature also means that they do not take themselves too seriously, and their sense of humour usually prevents them from holding back or being aloof for long. Above all, they are too open-minded, and too interested in life, to waste time in pretence or in being proud.

BORN UNDER THE DOGS: Hermann Hesse, Franz Kafka, Carl Jung, Sir Arthur Evans, Aldous Huxley, Sir Edmund Hillary, Raymond Chandler, Antoine de St-Exupéry, Nathaniel Hawthorne, John Glenn, Ernest Hemingway, Nelson Mandela, Stanley Spencer, Richard Branson, the Dalai Lama.

The Dogs and the Traditional Zodiac

June 28 – July 7, July 18–22   The Dogs and CANCER

These Dogs are gentler and more affectionate than those born under Leo. They are also more nostalgic for their past and more home-loving.

July 23–25   The Dogs and LEO

Those born under this combination are more adventurous and more one-track-minded than their Cancerian counterparts, and they are also more determined.

Relationships with Other 'Lost Zodiac' Signs

The Dogs with ORION
The Dogs are Orion's natural companions and loyal friends in life, as the Dogs can help Orion to come to terms with other people's values. They are more emotionally sophisticated than Orion, but, in turn, Orion never lets them down.

The Dogs with CROWN OF THE NORTH WIND
Both these signs are concerned with discovering what is hidden. The intellectual Crown can help the Dogs to make sense of what they find, while the Dogs offer the Crown instinctive wisdom, which it tends to lack.

The Dogs with the EAGLE
The high-soaring Eagle, who finds it so easy to see clearly, except in instinctive matters, needs the Dogs to help it find its way through the emotional maze, while the Eagle's lucid mind can help the Dogs to be more detached when they become too obsessed by an idea or a person.

THE SHIP OF THE ARGONAUTS
Argo Navis

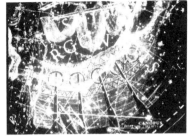

July 8–17 & September 22–28

GUIDING STARS: *July 8–17* is governed by **Canopus**, the main star in the great Ship, the *Argo*, which sails along the Milky Way, and is named after the pilot who steered the fleet home from Troy. The star was also worshipped in the Arabian deserts under the name 'Suhail', which means all that is bright, glorious and beautiful, on account of its 'blue, diamond brightness'. The word 'suhail' is still used by desert nomads to describe a handsome person. It is said to confer piety, immunity from disease, and the power to change evil to good.

Markeb, which rules those born between *September 22 and 28*, lies in the Ship's sail, and is seen as a fortunate and expansive star, which brings profit from journeys, and wide-ranging knowledge.

Both stars were once believed to protect those born under them from water.

PRECIOUS STONE: Sapphire
PLANT: Oak

The Legends

The story of Jason and the fifty Argonauts, and their quest for the Golden Fleece, is one of the most famous of the old Greek legends.

53

'Never before or since,' according to one ancient writer, 'was so gallant a ship's company gathered together', as the heroes who set sail in the *Argo*, probably sometime in the thirteenth century BC. Many of them had been brought up, like Jason, by the Wise Centaur, Chiron, who taught them all 'to shoot, to sing, to tell the truth', in his cave amongst the chestnut forests of Mount Pelion. He also taught them medicine, science, music, and, to Jason, he taught navigation by the stars. (For more on the Wise Centaur, see page 111.)

Jason, who had been sent to bring back the Golden Fleece from distant Colchis – modern Georgia – by his wicked uncle, who had usurped his kingdom, summoned his childhood friends to help him. The ship was built by the carpenter, Argus, and Athene, the grey-eyed goddess of reason, placed in its beam, to guide them, a piece of 'speaking oak' from Dodona, the oldest oracle in Greece, where the rustling leaves of the great, sacred oaks made prophecies. Amongst the fifty Argonauts were Orpheus, the legendary musician; Lynceus, who had superhuman sight; Caeneus, who had once been a woman; Zetes and Calais, the sons of the North Wind; Castor and Polydeuces (or Pollux), the Heavenly Twins of Gemini, Mopsus, who had second sight and could understand the language of the birds, Hercules (or Heracles), the strongest man the world has ever known and his beautiful friend, Hylas. Jason himself has been described as being fatally handsome – like the star, Suhail or Canopus.

On the way to distant Colchis they had many battles and adventures. In Lemnos, for instance, they slept with all the women, who had murdered their husbands for accusing them of smelling. In Samothrace, they were initiated into the mysteries of the underworld, and in the Bosphorus they danced, fully armed, and clashed their shields to placate Asia's great earth goddess. They saved Phineas, who had been cursed for prophesying the future too well, from the dreadful Harpies, and navigated Russian ice-floes in the Black Sea, where, Apollo, the god of prophecy and music, appeared to them in a blaze of glory; finally, having fought off great flocks of migrating birds with brazen plumes, they arrived in Colchis.

There, Medea, the king's daughter, whose name means 'cunning' and 'knowing', fell in love with the handsome Jason. Her father, understandably, had no desire to part with the legendary Fleece, and set Jason a number of apparently impossible tasks, but luckily for Jason, Medea was a witch and a devotee of Hecate, the goddess of the underworld. With Medea's help, Jason was triumphant. The first task he was set by the king of Colchis was to yoke two bronze-hoofed, fire-breathing bulls and plough a field with them: anointed with the blood-red juice of the dangerous Caucasian crocus, which Medea gave him, he miraculously succeeded. He then had to sow the field with dragons' teeth, which sprouted from the earth as warriors, fully armed and fighting, which he also overcame. But Medea's father still refused to give up the Fleece, and so, by night, Jason and Medea crept into the sacred grove, where it hung from a tree, guarded by a watchful dragon. With sprigs of juniper and incantations, Medea lulled the monstrous being to sleep, and they fled back to the waiting ship carrying their glimmering trophy.

To save themselves, they cruelly tricked and killed Medea's brother – a crime, according to the piece of speaking oak, for which they must be purified by the powerful witch, Circe, who was Medea's aunt. Even Circe, who thought nothing of turning men to swine, was horrified, but reluctantly absolved them. Even so, Jason was not destined to become king in his uncle's place, and so, at last, they ended up in distant Corinth. There, they made their home and had two children, but, after ten years of marriage, Jason betrayed Medea and took up with Glauce, the daughter of the powerful king of Corinth. Medea, in revenge, sent the new bride a poisoned wedding dress, which engulfed her in a supernatural fire that could never be extinguished. Having murdered her rival, she then cut the throats of her own two children, and whirled out of Corinth in a chariot drawn by dragons, belonging to her grandfather, the sun.

Jason lingered on in Corinth, dreaming of his glorious and adventurous past, until, one day, while he sat beneath the shade of the great ship which had carried all the heroes, he was killed by the speaking piece of oak, which fell on him from the rotten bows.

The Star Sign

The Ship is the most gifted – and versatile – sign in the heavens. 'Never before or since, was so gallant a ship's company gathered together', and, like the crew of the *Argo*, who between them had so many talents, those born under its glimmering, southern stars can turn their hand, quite literally, to anything, if they choose to do so.

They are natural leaders, and, like Argus, who built the ship, they can be inspired craftsmen. Like Orpheus, they are often artists and musicians. They have sharp insight and a powerful intuition, and, like Caeneus, who had once been a woman, they can understand, and relate to, the outlook of the other sex. They are often also natural athletes, like the Heavenly Twins, and, to cap it all, they usually have great charm, good looks, and a healthy constitution.

They can have anything, or anyone, they want, but, of course, there has to be a down side. Where most heroes know what dragons they are up against, those born under the Great Ship have to overcome their own laziness and ambition, an insidious combination, just as dangerous as any dragon. They set their sights high, but, because life has been so generous to them, they are not used to making an effort, and they quite easily give up. They can, in short, be spoilt, and often fall back on their persuasive charms to get their way, instead of using their great talents in a life-enhancing and creative manner. They may be the nicest people, and often are, but if they are not careful, and always choose the soft option, lapsing into subterfuge and cunning, like Medea, they can slowly lose their sense of right and wrong.

The hardest thing, then, for those born under the Great Ship, for whom life seems so easy, is to keep their hands firmly on the rudder and navigate their chosen course, without relying too much on charm, or on other people. If they can overcome these failings, they are also less likely to fall prey to the Medea type in life. Medea, the 'cunning' and 'knowing', can usually see them coming from afar, and will use their weakness to gain power over them. Although Jason is not evil, he can be naïve and easily led astray – especially when he has set his sights on the Golden Fleece, which still remains a symbol for the almost unattainable in life.

But they have another option, which can transform their lives. The Ship's crew may be a reflection of their many gifts and talents, and Medea of their weaker and more devious side, but the piece of 'speaking oak', which was built into the beam, represents the voice of their true inner self. Everyone is tempted to ignore it at times, because it does not always point out the easiest way, but for those born under the Great Ship, who seem to have so much else they can rely on, this temptation is far greater. If, however, they can learn to listen to the still, small voice, instead of to Medea, and steer the course which it dictates across the sea of life, they can survive the wildest storms unscathed. A lot may be asked of them, but, then, they have more gifts and advantages than those born under most other signs, and are more than capable of rising to the challenge.

Once they have set the Ship on its true course, things start to fall into place, as though by magic, and new avenues open, both in their relationships with other people, and in their careers. Then they attract people who like them for themselves, instead of for their looks and charm, and who, instead of using them, like Medea, will respect their freedom and help them to make the most of their creative powers. And, as we have seen, they can succeed at anything they turn their hand to, if they try.

At every stage of life's journey, they can also count on their close friends, as they are always popular and their sense of comradeship – and loyalty – is unrivalled. Until they transcend the Medea phase in their more personal relationships, however, they can feel more at home with friendship – which always means so much to them – than with love and romance, where happiness often comes only later. Their ideal relationship is usually based on comradeship – and freedom. They are, after all, the great adventurers and explorers, and, if they are to get the best from life, they need the freedom to explore, to experience and to enjoy as many facets of existence as they can.

BORN UNDER THE SHIP: Alexandre Dumas (author of *The Three Musketeers*), Captain Maryatt, Emmeline Pankhurst, Jacqueline Onassis, Marcel Proust, Erle Stanley Gardner, F. Scott Fitzgerald, Mark Rothko, William Faulkner, T. S. Eliot, Bryan Ferry, Marcello Mastroianni, Brigitte Bardot, Miguel de Cervantes, Horatio Lord Nelson, Roald Amundsen, Baroness Orczy, Walter Lippman, Felicia Hemans (author of 'Casabianca' – 'The boy stood on the burning deck . . .')

The Great Ship and the Traditional Zodiac

July 8–17   The Great Ship and CANCER
The Great Ship and Cancer, the crab which lives on the shores of the ocean, are both watery signs and have a strong affiliation with the sea. The influence of the Ship helps the shy and sensitive Crab to be more out-going, and makes these Cancerians far less home-loving and more adventurous than others. Because this area of the heavens, through which the sun passes in midsummer, is so full of large and powerful stars, those born under the great Ship in July are also influenced by the Dog Stars (see page 47).

September 22–28   The Ship and LIBRA
Those born under the Ship who are also influenced by Libra are less emotional than those born under Cancer. Their quest is also more likely to be on the intellectual level.

Relationships With Other 'Lost Zodiac' Signs

The Great Ship with THE LYRE OF ORPHEUS
They share a love of art and music, and are staunch allies to one another. Orpheus also brings out both the Ship's romantic and ambitious nature.

The Great Ship with THE RIVER
Apart from both being water signs, these two share a sense of adventure, a need for freedom, and often a common goal.

The Great Ship with THE WISE CENTAUR
Chiron, the Wise Centaur who brought up Jason, and taught him the art of navigation by the stars, often plays the role of guide and mentor to those born under the Ship.

The Great Ship also has a bond with all the other watery signs: the Swan, the Sea Serpent, and the Dolphin.

THE DRAGON
Draco

July 26–August 7 & December 17–23

GUIDING STARS: *July 26 – August 7* Governing those born between these dates are **Gianfar,** which marks the Dragon's tail, and **Kochab,** an orange giant, which now lies in the constellation of Ursa Minor, the Little Bear, marking what was once the Dragon's vanished wing; now known as the Guardian of the Pole, Kochab was the Pole Star itself around 3,000 years ago.

Grumium, marking the Dragon's jaw, and **Etanin,** which marks its ear, rule the dates *December 17–23.*

PRECIOUS STONE: Magnet, Lode-stone
PLANT: Tarragon

The Legends

The eleventh labour of the mighty hero, Hercules (or Heracles), took him to the far west of the world. There, in the land of the setting sun, beyond Oceanus, the great River of Time which the Greeks believed encircled the whole earth like a huge serpent, there lay a legendary garden. The garden was, in turn, encircled by a river called the Ladon, and belonged to the Hesperides, the sweetly singing nymphs who were the daughters of the Evening Star and of Atlas, the giant who held the heavens on his shoulders, and who grazed his flocks nearby.

It was the hero's task to steal the golden apples of immortality which grew there – the gift of Gaia, the earth goddess, to Hera on her marriage. These were closely guarded by Atlas and his daughters, as well as by a dragon, whose name was Ladon, like the river which snaked around the magical, walled garden. Ladon, who lay coiled around the tree of immortality, was ever-watchful and spoke in 'divers tongues'. To obtain the apples, Hercules played a cruel trick on Atlas, 'the long-suffering one', who was the first astronomer and knew so much about the heavens that he 'carried' the entire celestial sphere upon his shoulders. So heavy was it that it was not hard for Hercules to persuade him to pick the apples for him while he, Hercules, shouldered the globe for a short while; as Atlas was afraid of Ladon, Hercules killed him with an arrow through the heart. Atlas, having tasted freedom, was loath to take his burden on his shoulders once again, but when he came back with the apples, Hercules managed to trick him into holding it 'for a moment', laughed and walked away. Hera, the queen of the gods, meanwhile, was overcome with grief at the death of Ladon, the guardian of her apples, and placed him amongst the stars. There, he lies alongside Hercules, guarding the North Pole, 'the still point in the turning world', which is the symbolic doorway between this world and the next, where he is 'ever-vigilant because he never sets'.

Like Oceanus – the serpentine River of Time which divides this world from the beyond – the dragon, Ladon, is both serpent and river, guarding the treasure of immortality in the timeless, sunset garden in the west, the land of death. The golden apples have been believed by some to be the golden clouds of sunset, with their immortal promise, which were thought of, in those days, as the 'celestial flocks' of heaven. These are shepherded across the evening sky – the first astronomer's starry garden – by the daughters of the Evening Star, the first to shine as the sun sets.

Our word 'dragon' is related to the Greek word 'drakos', meaning 'eye', and, like Ladon, dragons are legendary for their vigilance. In the ancient world, the dragon was the Dweller on the Threshold, the guardian of temple sanctuaries, of hoards of jewels, or of the Golden Fleece, who must be conquered or outwitted before the hero wins the longed-for prize.

The dragon is also a symbol of the teeming and chaotic fertility of nature, of the fire and rain and lightning which bring both life and destruction to the world. In the West this force, which mankind struggles to combat and control, but without which he cannot survive, has been seen as evil, for the most part, and so our mythology abounds with stories of bold dragon-slayers, like St Michael and St George. From the West, also, comes the vision of the dragon as a symbol of our inner darkness, which, if we would triumph and win immortality, we must fight and overcome. But the Dragon was not always regarded as evil, even in the West: in our earliest creation myth, predating Babylon, the whole of life was born from Tiamat, the great she-dragon of chaos. Only later was she seen as a dark and sinister being which must be conquered by the hero, who stands for light, reason and control.

In China, however, it has always been a very different story. There, the dragon stands for heavenly, spiritual power and wisdom, as well as for the magnetic currents which are considered to fertilize the earth. These are called 'lung mei', and are similar to Western 'ley-lines'.

Both Eastern and Western philosophies can be found in the Celtic tale of Merlin, who as a child was asked why the tower of King Vortigern kept falling down however often it was mended and rebuilt. Merlin replied that beneath the tower's foundations two dragons – symbolizing the earth's virility and power – were fighting. This meant that only a true king could tame the powers of the land he ruled – and Vortigern could not.

The Star Sign

The Dragon is one of the noblest and most powerful of the ancient signs, and there is nothing small-minded – or cosy – about those born beneath this fiery symbol of the life-force and the imagination. Ladon, the dragon in the stars, is the Dweller on the Threshold who guards the doorway to eternity. Through this doorway all new things also come into this world, which makes those born beneath the Dragon the natural guardians of the creative process and the custodians of art and beauty. These things mean much more to them than comfort and security, which they can manage without better than most other signs.

As their aesthetic sense is so well-developed, they do like to be surrounded by nice things, however – like the dragon with its hoard of gold and jewels – and man-made things mean more to them than the wonders of the natural world. This is not because they do not see and appreciate them, but because the products of the human spirit, such as churches, jewellery and paintings, seem more miraculous, and so more valuable, to them.

On the whole, those born under the Dragon fall into two types: those who are themselves creative, and those who nurture creativity in others, or perform the role of guardians. The second type, of course, rarely achieves the fame and glory of the first; but this is not important to them, as they are more concerned with what they are nurturing than they are with personal recognition. This is true of both types – what counts is not the singer but the song.

They can also be quite solitary, preferring to spend their time looking and learning to being in the stream of life. Their thirst for knowledge and their breadth of vision ensure that they do not easily grow bored without others to amuse them. They are private people who like, and need, a domain of their own, into which they can retire when the mood takes them.

Despite the need for their own territory and for solitude, they also need close relationships with others. The Dragon is a symbol of the life-force, and those born beneath its stars have powerful emotions which they must express in order to be happy and fulfilled. Because they feel so strongly, it can be hard for them to be detached, especially when young, and unfounded jealousy can be a problem for them. When anything goes wrong in a relationship, they tend to fear the worst, and, rather than asking direct questions, and discovering that their fears are groundless, they tend to hide behind their pride – and anger. It can take a lot of insight – and courage – on the part of those with whom they are involved to calm them down again, for the Dragon is a fiery creature when it is aroused. For the most part, however, they are far less fierce than they are painted, and are loyal and stalwart friends.

As time goes by, they also learn to distance themselves from their emotions. For the Dragon, unlike its earthly counterpart, the Serpent, has wings to help it rise above the storm and see its problems in perspective, and it is often in solitude that it achieves this.

It is then that those born beneath its stars also discover how to express themselves not through relationships alone, but through creativity. This ability to stand back and to transform their fiery feelings into art or music makes their lives more peaceful and fulfilling, and teaches them to respect others who are doing, or have done, the same. Their fieriness can also be employed in helping others to create something of worth or beauty, and no one is then more fiercely protective – or encouraging – than they are.

Thanks to its passionate and fiery nature, a Dragon's life may not always be plain sailing, but it is full of meaning, and of beauty, which to the brave Dragon, are worth more than anything.

BORN UNDER THE DRAGON: Isaac Newton, Paul Klee, Alfred Lord Tennyson, Rupert Brooke, Herman Melville, James Baldwin, Stanley Kubrick, J. Arthur Rank, Steven Spielberg, Mick Jagger, Keith Richards, John Huston, Peter O'Toole, Edith Piaf, Yves St-Laurent,

Henry Moore, Marcel Duchamp, Uri Geller, Emily Brontë, Percy Bysshe Shelley.

The Dragon and the Traditional Zodiac

July 26 – August 7   The Dragon and LEO
The combined influence of these two royal and powerful beings makes these Leos easily the proudest and most fiery. They are a force to be reckoned with, and tend to be the most creative Dragons.

December 17–21   The Dragon and SAGITTARIUS
These Dragons are quite similar to those born under Leo, but they are more idealistic and less proud.

December 22–23   The Dragon and CAPRICORN
Those born under the Dragon and the earthy and ambitious sign of Capricorn are more practical – and more introverted – as well as more likely to achieve their goals.

Relationships with Other 'Lost Zodiac' Signs

The Dragon with THE SERPENT
These two have much in common, but the Dragon lacks the Serpent's guile and love of intrigue. It can, however, enable the Serpent to be more balanced and objective, while the Serpent helps the Dragon by being more truthful and direct than it is with most other signs.

The Dragon with THE CHARIOTEER
The Charioteer's cool, intellectual approach to life helps the Dragon to see clearly and be more detached, while the Dragon sees, and understands, the Charioteer's emotional side and can help him to come to terms with it.

The Dragon with THE CUP
The Cup's easygoing fun-loving nature is relaxing to the Dragon,

helping it to take life less seriously, while the companionable Cup can learn discrimination from the choosier Dragon.

THE GREAT BEAR
Ursa Major

August 8–15 & August 24–September 10

GUIDING STARS: Those born between *August 8 and 15* are governed by **Dubhe** and **Merak,** the two stars known as 'the pointers' as they point to the North Pole.

People born *August 24–September 10* are ruled by **Phekda, Megrez, Alioth** and **Mizar,** which lie along the Great Bear's tail and form the handle of the Plough, or Big Dipper.

PRECIOUS STONE: Moonstone

PLANT: Willow

The Legends

The stars of the Great Bear, which circles round the north celestial pole, and which form the brightest and best-known constellation in the northern skies, have been seen as a bear from Babylon to ancient India, and from Greece to the North American plains. To the ancient Greeks, this constellation represented Callisto, a nymph of the mountainous kingdom of Arcadia, who was a follower of Artemis, the virgin huntress and the goddess of the crescent moon. Artemis demanded the strictest chastity from the maidens who spent their lives hunting through the mountains and bathing in the crystal streams with her; but Callisto was seduced by Zeus, who took on the form of Artemis to deceive her. Some say that Zeus transformed

Callisto into the Great Bear and set her in the stars, with Arcas, their child, beside her, to save them from the wrath of the virgin goddess. Others claim, however, that it was either Artemis or Hera who, in rage, cursed Callisto, who then turned into a bear and was pursued by her own hounds, only later to be placed amongst the stars. Arcas, her child, grew up to be Arcadia's king, bringing agriculture to that wild and rugged country, for which he was immortalized amongst the stars as Boötes, the inventor of the Wagon, which is the other name for the stars of the Great Bear. (For the legends of Boötes, which should be read as well by anyone born under the Great Bear, see the Bear-Keeper on page 91.)

Behind the story of Callisto, however, lies a far more ancient belief. For the Great Bear is really Artemis herself, and Callisto, 'the best', or 'the most beautiful' is another name for Artemis. She is the ancient queen of the stars and the she-bear is her symbol.

Artemis was known in Greece as 'the Lady of the Wild Mountains' and 'the Sounding One', whose voice was heard in the rustling leaves of the forests, and in the sound of birds and animals and bees in solitary places. She was the queen of the 'inviolate meadow', far from the haunts of men, as well as of the crescent moon, and she gave off a 'brilliant blaze' as she hunted through the mountains; moonlight was her actual presence and was believed to cause wild animals and trees to dance.

But it is her connection with the bear, which has been considered sacred since at least 75,000 BC – before the Ice Age – which makes Artemis easily the most ancient of all the goddesses of Greece. And, in ancient Greece, 3,000 years ago, young girls, who came under her especial care as the virgin goddess, still danced, dressed as bears, in honour of the old bear-goddess.

Centuries later, the early English also linked this glittering constellation to both the Bear and Wagon. They saw it as the home, or as the bier, or the wagon of the legendary King Arthur, whose Round Table is reflected in the constellations circling the Pole, and whose name some say comes from the Celtic word for 'bear'. And, as King Arthur lay dying after his last battle, a bier appeared, containing three mysterious, immortal queens to take him across the water to the other-world of Avalon, where they would heal his wounds.

Legend also has it that Arthur is not dead, but sleeping in a cave inside a mountain, with his knights beside him, and that he will return one day to save his country in its hour of need. Even this part of his story is reflected in the stars, for the seven most important stars of the Bear-Wagon are also known as the Seven Sleepers of Ephesus, who lie dreaming, like King Arthur, in a mountain cave, waiting for the resurrection. Unlike King Arthur and his knights, however, they are said to have awoken after two hundred years and gone down to the local town to get provisions, after which they went to sleep once more.

Arthur, the 'Once and Future King', then, has many links with the far more ancient Arcas, the 'bear' king and son of the great goddess, Artemis, who rules the Arctic Pole.

The Star Sign

Of all the ancient signs beyond the zodiac, the Great Bear, which dominates the Northern Pole, is the grandest and most powerful. This is the 'royal sign', as can be seen from the long list of monarchs and great statesmen born beneath its stars. It is queen of all that it surveys, as it circles slowly round the Pole, and those born under it, even the many who do not hold the reins of power, are always personalities built on a grand scale. There is nothing mean or petty about their outlook on the world, and they pride themselves on their breadth of vision. 'Renaissance man', who knew enough about most subjects to ensure he had a rounded view of life, is their ideal, and they have no time for those who concentrate on just one field. This can put them at a disadvantage in the modern world, although usually they are more than able to look after themselves. They have strength and courage, as well as an instinctive understanding of other people, which makes it easy for them to delegate dull tasks. The details of daily existence bore them because their minds work best when engaged on the grand scheme of things. As a result, they may seem lazy, but they are not pretentious and they admire true soul and simplicity far more than sophistication. In fact, unless worldly power and wealth are thrust upon them, they would far rather go without the luxuries of life than waste time and energy pursuing meaningless and trivial things. When they need to, though, they can motivate large groups of people – and win loyalty and support through thick and thin – with alarming ease.

They do not waste words and there is usually a great deal more going on inside their heads than they admit as they also have a solitary side. Both the bear and the virgin goddess, who were worshipped as one, are loners, and those born beneath the Great Bear's stars never follow the herd blindly. They need space, solitude and contact with the wildnesses of nature to make them feel relaxed and whole – and to give them time to see life in the round. Without room to breathe, they can become bad-tempered – for which bears, of course, are famous – and anyone who trespasses on their private, inner realm can expect to receive short shrift. And one blow from a bear's paw, as everybody knows, can bring a strong man down. But usually they do not mean to hurt others and often do not realize how devastating their ill-humour can be to those who come too close when they want to be alone. Beneath their gruff exterior, they are kindly and affectionate people, and, when they are feeling sociable, they show quite a different side to their nature. Then, they are the soul of warmth and generosity and it is thanks to their great charm and humour – and their approachability – at such times that they are so popular and can make so many loyal and lifelong friends. Even though they can be moody, they are honest, so that you always know exactly where you are with them, for good or bad. They may not *say* what they are thinking, but they do show their real emotions at all times. They are also very loyal, in turn, to anyone with whom they form a true bond, and friendship is important to them, as are their children, to whom they dedicate a great deal of energy and time.

Affectionate, loyal and honest they may be, with a sardonic sense of humour but, to understand them, it is necessary also to understand why they sometimes need to be alone. The bear, as we have seen, is a symbol of the ancient virgin goddess, who was independent, free and self-contained. She stands for the inner wholeness which does not need to rely on others for meaning and fulfilment. That wholeness is the true life-goal of those born under the Great Bear. This does not mean, of course, that they are always aware of their purpose, nor does it mean that they do not form relationships with others. But it does mean that they are independent and self-sufficient. They need freedom and they respect that need in others. They have a natural understanding that the winds of heaven must always be allowed to blow between them and those with whom they are involved – otherwise no one concerned can change and grow.

BORN UNDER THE GREAT BEAR: Napoleon Bonaparte, Richard Coeur de Lion, King Henry V, Queen Elizabeth I, King Louis XIV, Ivan the Terrible, Cardinal Richelieu, Camillo Cavour, Fidel Castro, T. E. Lawrence, the 'Grand Old Duke of York', Annie Oakley, Grandma Moses, Raquel Welch, Mother Teresa, Ingrid Bergman, Cecil B. De Mille, Leo Tolstoy, Johann Wolfgang Goethe, Van Morrison, Davy Crockett, Otis Redding, Peter Sellers, King George IV.

The Great Bear and the Traditional Zodiac

August 8–15   The Great Bear and LEO
Those born beneath the combined influence of the Great Bear and Leo are more regal and flamboyant than those born under Virgo – or, indeed, than anyone else. Thanks to the Lion, King of Beasts, which brings these traits so strongly to the fore, they have a double dose of power and grandeur, and are extroverts who are a force to be reckoned with.

August 24–September 10   The Great Bear and VIRGO
The influence of Virgo brings out the more introverted, solitary side of the Great Bear, and life is more a spiritual quest for wholeness than it is for those born under the flamboyant sign of Leo. They are also gentler than the Leo type.

Relationships with Other 'Lost Zodiac' Signs

The Great Bear with THE BEAR KEEPER
The Great Bear's deepest bonds are often formed with the Bear Keeper. This can be a love relationship, but often they are linked by common goals, the Bear Keeper putting into action the grand plan of the Great Bear. They also share a need for peace and solitude, which makes this a harmonious combination.

The Great Bear with ORION
The giant huntsman, Orion, and the Great Bear are both built on a grand scale and they share a need and love for freedom and open spaces. Orion was the only love of Artemis, the virgin goddess, and it is often among those born beneath the Golden Huntsman's stars that the Great Bear finds true love and fulfilment.

The Great Bear with the SERPENT
The Serpent is another sign which has strong links with the Great Goddess, so there is often a natural understanding between those born beneath these signs. It can be more of a love–hate relationship, however, as the Serpent lacks the Bear's honesty and directness, and this can lead to suspicion and mistrust between them.

THE SEA SERPENT
Hydra

August 16–23

GUIDING STAR: **Alphard,** the Solitary One, rules the lives of those born between *August 16 and 23.* This orange star, which marks the heart of the Hydra, or Sea Serpent, the largest constellation in the sky, was believed by early astrologers to bestow a love of art and music, strong passions and some wisdom, especially about human nature. The Sea Serpent, whose winding course once symbolized the path of the moon, was seen in Babylon as 'the source of the fountains of the deep'.

PRECIOUS STONE: Lapis lazuli.

PLANT: Sea-holly (*Eryngium maritimum*)

The Legends

Long before Babylon was built, about 4,000 years ago, the goddess, Nammu, was worshipped in the 'fertile crescent' of Sumeria, where civilization first began, between the river Tigris and the broad Euphrates. Nammu, the Great Mother, personified the primordial ocean from which all life emerged, and the sea serpent was her symbol. By Babylonian times, however, the sun-gods had replaced the ancient mother goddess, whom they called Tiamat, the she-dragon of chaos and the salty ocean. By then she had come to be seen as evil and a force that needed to be slain and overcome by solar gods and heroes. The Babylonian creation myth, the *Enuma Elish*, describes how she met her end at the hands of her great-great-great grandson, Marduk, who is the prototype for all the dragon-slayers, like St Michael and St George, who followed after. This story, in which the feminine principle, which had once been viewed as the benign source of life, is seen as destructive, demonic and chaotic, and something to be feared and overcome, formed the basis for the great patriarchal religions of Judaism, Christianity and Islam.

In the Christian world, Leviathan, the terrifying monster of the deep with which Jehovah struggles in the Bible, is probably the best-known of these great sea serpents.

Not all serpents were viewed as evil everywhere, however. For the Aztecs and the Mayans, for example, Quetzalcoatl, the Plumed Serpent, was the creator god who gave breath and brought rain. Later, the Serpent god was seen as an ancient and benevolent king, who had come to teach agriculture, religion, art, crafts and weaving to the people. It was thanks to their belief that Quetzalcoatl had departed eastwards across the ocean on a raft of serpents, but would one day return, like King Arthur, that the Aztecs surrendered to Cortes and the Spaniards when they came.

In west Africa, the serpent is also a positive being. There, it is the Rainbow Snake, or divine python, that supports the weight of the whole world, around which it lies with its tail in its mouth. If it loosened its coils, the world would fall apart, but, except for an occasional wriggle, which is the cause of earthquakes, it lies mercifully still.

The same idea of a great cosmic serpent, encircling the earth with its tail in its mouth is also found in Ancient Greece and in Scandinavia. In Greece, this mighty serpent-river is Oceanus, the serpentine River of Time, which girdled the earth, just as the zodiac girdled the sky. The Ourobouros, a round serpent with its tail in its mouth, is still a symbol of the cycle of time, life, death and rebirth. Midgard, the middle-earth of the Norse world, was also surrounded by one, known as the Serpent of Midgard. There, however, the sea serpent, with which Thor, the thunder-god, did battle, is seen as a destructive force, perhaps because the Viking universe is war-like and male.

Last but not least of the great sea serpents are those which still continue to haunt mankind's imagination – if not the world itself. The Loch Ness monster is probably the most famous of the mysterious sea serpents, which have been 'sighted' the world over. It is, however, not the largest, or the fiercest of these strange beings, which, by all accounts, can measure up to 600 feet in length and snatch men from the decks of boats. Whether they exist may not, of course, ever be discovered, but the descriptions are detailed and varied: 'The head in all kinds has a high and broad forehead, but in some a pointed snout, though in others that is flat like that of a cow or horse, with large nostrils, and several stiff hairs standing out on each side like whiskers', wrote a Norwegian bishop in the mid-eighteenth century. He continues: 'The eyes of this creature are very large, and of a blue colour, like a couple of bright pewter plates. It is speckled and variegated with light streaks and spots that shine like tortoiseshell.' And they appear, it would seem, only when the sea is calm, during the warm 'Dog Days', which stretch from mid-July to early August.

The Star Sign

As water is the element of feeling and emotion in astrology, those born beneath the stars of the sea serpent, whose winding course once symbolized the pathway of the wandering moon which rules the tides, are more at home in the watery realm of feeling than any other sign, except, perhaps, the zodiac sign of Pisces.

This does not mean that they are always calm, however. This is the sign of the sea, and the range of their emotions is as wide and fast-moving as the ocean, which can be as smooth as a sheet of glass, and then, without warning can turn stormy and start crashing on the shore. But the storm usually soon passes of its own accord, and, even though they may be volatile, not far beneath the surface they are not really that disturbed, as they have a natural and instinctive faith in life and in the future, and are not afraid of change or the unknown.

It is in solitude that those born under the influence of Alphard, the Solitary One, often find it easiest to tune into these deeper waters which are not disturbed by passing storms. They live a great deal through their senses, and the sounds and colours which surround them are so real and vivid to them that they can happily spend days on end enjoying the pleasures of the moment on their own. But they have no wish to isolate themselves unless they feel rejected. They are tactile, sensuous and erotic, and they need human contact to feel good about themselves; at the same time it can be hard for them to understand other people's boundaries and inhibitions, as they have so few themselves.

To live in this world, however, some boundaries are essential – a fact which those born under the Sea Serpent, which personifies the boundless ocean, need to come to terms with if they are to find contentment and relate successfully to others. Until they manage to develop a more separate sense of self, they can be too open, trusting the wrong people, which means that they get hurt – and, when they are, they quickly vanish back into their private inner world. This is the ocean of the senses and emotions where there are no manmade boundaries to confuse them, and so they feel at home.

As time goes by, however, they learn to be more cautious, and so they are less vulnerable and more balanced in their dealings with the world. And, because they have been subject to such a wide range of moods, they become subtle and sophisticated when dealing with emotions of all kinds.

This is also when they can begin to tap the source of their creative powers – for which the ocean is a symbol – instead of merely plunging deep beneath the waves to hide. For the Sea Serpent, which, in ancient Babylon, was believed to be 'the source of the fountains of the Great Deep', is one of the most creative of all signs once the waters start to flow. They then excel at anything which makes use of their well-developed eye – and ear – for beauty, as well as of their sense of humour and their natural ability to enjoy life to the full. They do have a tendency, however, to indulge their senses, and their love of pleasure, luxury and comfort can sometimes go well into the realm of excess, as can their self-pity. But their generosity of spirit, and the fact that they are, mostly, such fun to be with, more than makes up for their failings. Above all, they are tolerant and warm-hearted and they expect the same from others in return, as life, according to their way of thinking, is too precious, and too short, to waste on being disapproving or unkind.

BORN UNDER THE SEA SERPENT: Aubrey Beardsley, Ted Hughes, Claude Debussy, Coco Chanel, Max Beerbohm, Dorothy Parker, Cartier Bresson, V. S. Naipaul, Karlheinz Stockhausen, Jack Teagarden, George Melly, Madonna, Mae West, Robert de Niro, Robert Redford.

The Sea Serpent and the Traditional Zodiac

August 16–23   The Sea Serpent and LEO
These Leos are more fun-loving and emotional – and less autocratic – than those born under the Great Bear or the Dragon. They are also more concerned with comfort and material possessions.

Relationships with Other 'Lost Zodiac' Signs

The Sea Serpent with the DOLPHIN
These two sea-creatures are both sensual and artistic. They can have lots of fun together and empathize with one another, but their shared dislike of limitations and routine can mean that they play too hard and achieve too little.

The Sea Serpent with CROWN OF THE NORTH WIND
The natural spontaneity of those born under the Sea Serpent, and their ability to live life simply in the moment, make them ideal companions for the complex and sophisticated Crown, who needs simplicity, and enjoys their easygoing company.

The Sea Serpent with ANDROMEDA
While those born under Andromeda tend to be too hidebound by conventions, especially when young, the Sea Serpent hardly seems to notice such conventions, which can be liberating for the chained princess. In return, Andromeda can teach them how to understand what the world expects of them, which makes life easier for them.

THE CUP OF DIONYSUS
Crater

September 11–21

GUIDING STAR: For people born between *September 11–21* it is **Alkes,** the brightest in the constellation of the wine god Dionysus's Cup. It is a yellow giant, 160 light-years distant, and it can be seen in spring in the northern hemisphere, low on the southern horizon.

PRECIOUS STONE: Amethyst

PLANTS: Ivy and Vine

The Legends

Zeus, the king of the gods, loved Semele, the daughter of the king of Thebes, whose name means 'moon'. Foolishly she pleaded with Zeus to show himself to her in all his glory, a request which he could not refuse, though the blinding light reduced her to a pile of ashes, from which Zeus plucked their unborn child. This child was Dionysus, the young God of liberation and libation, wine and ecstasy, who was horned and crowned with serpents, and who, because of the jealousy of Hera, Zeus's wife, was brought up in secret as a girl.

When he grew to manhood, Hera acknowledged him as Zeus's son, but drove him mad and he then wandered through the world with a retinue of centaurs, fauns and satyrs, and women who wore faun-skins and wreaths of ivy, drinking wine and playing on flutes and tambourines. Dionysus's first port of call was Egypt, to which he introduced the vine, and where he helped the Amazons to defeat the giant Titans. From there, the wine god went to India, throwing a bridge of vines and ivy over the broad Euphrates, and crossing the Tigris on a tiger sent by his father, Zeus. Dionysus, and wine, soon conquered India and he returned to Europe, in triumph, with elephants and leopards added to his train.

The travels of Dionysus tell us, in the language of myth, about the real history of the spread of wine-making in the ancient world, and, true to fact, Greece itself was one of the last places where it was introduced. There, in the sixth century BC, an ancient poem tells us, Dionysus, when drowsy with wine, was kidnapped by a pirate ship which was travelling across 'the waste of wine-dark waters' on its way to Asia. One of the sailors, however, sensed that this man, dressed in purple, 'his raven hair tossing about his shoulders' was a god and pleaded with his comrades to treat the stranger with respect and set him free. They refused, but soon regretted it, for suddenly, 'through their black ship gushed streams of wine' and a divine and awe-inspiring fragrance filled the air. Vines heavy with grapes grew up the rigging on all sides and 'dark coils of winding ivy, bright with flowers and berries' coiled around the mast. Frozen where they stood, the sailors stared as the oars turned into green and twisting serpents, and, to the sound of flutes, phantom beasts, appearing from the shadows, prowled across the deck. A shaggy bear, 'aloft in fury', preceded Dionysus, himself now transformed into a lion. He gave a thunderous roar and the sailors who had not acknowledged him dived overboard and were changed to dolphins. Dionysus was kind, however, to the sailor who had tried to save him.

As can be seen from this ancient story, Dionysus could bring not only joy but terror to mankind, especially to those who attempted to deny his power, like Pentheus, king of Thebes, murdered by the wine god's followers, who tore him limb from limb.

On his return from India, Dionysus stopped on the Isle of Naxos. There, he found the Cretan princess, Ariadne, weeping on the shore, having been abandoned by Theseus. Dionysus and Ariadne were soon married, to the sound of drums and flutes and tambourines, and her wedding crown, of gold and Indian rubies, was placed by him amongst the stars as the Northern Crown or the Crown of the North Wind. Dionysus, having taken Greece by storm, was then, according to some legends, made into one of the twelve chief gods of Mount Olympus, taking the throne of Hestia, the quiet goddess of the hearth and home.

The constellation of the Cup, or Goblet, was also linked by the Greeks with Apollo, the bright god of prophecy and music.

It is also the cup of the Indian Dionysus, Soma, who is not only the moon, but also the magical plant, soma, as well as the elixir of immortal life made from it, which inspired both gods and men with ecstasy and poetic frenzy. Like Dionysus, Soma could appear in many forms; he is a giant of the waters, the king of plants, a bird, an embryo, a celestial bull and the cure for all evil.

Last but not least, these stars represent the Holy Grail, the cup which caught Christ's blood and which can bring spiritual illumination and new life to a blighted and decaying world.

The Star Sign

For those born beneath the glimmering goblet of the wine god, life is there to be lived to the full and to be enjoyed. They are the life and soul of any group of people and rarely spend much time alone, as they thrive on company. They are free spirits, who resent limitations or constraints of any kind and have little time for structure or routine; and what little money they have they would rather spend on pleasure than on dull necessities.

Without freedom and space, they can soon become bad-tempered and depressed, as, unlike more solemn, sober signs, they genuinely need to let their hair down and enjoy what life has got on offer. Like Dionysus, who was the youngest of the gods, they have a natural, youthful *joie de vivre* and sense of humour, and they do best in occupations in which they can allow these life-enhancing qualities free rein. As they are such fun to be with, they are not usually short of friends to help them out in times of need, but they are also more than able to look after themselves, when they have to, as they are quick-witted and creative.

The main problem with the Dionysian temperament, however, is its tendency to overdo things, and however much they have of something, whether it is love, or wine, or laughter, they usually want more. But when they get it – which they tend to do, as they spare no effort when it comes to satisfying their whims and desires – they are often disappointed. This does not stop them – at least to begin with – from repeating the same pattern, but sooner or later their desires, and their overall life-view, undergo a change, as it is not really pleasure, pure and simple, that they thirst after. For, deep down, beneath their hedonistic and carefree exterior, they are quite serious people. Just at Dionysus was not only the god of wine and song, but of ecstatic union with all life, so those born beneath the Cup, which also represents the Holy Grail, are motivated by a real need to find fulfilment, and to feel at one with life. Being isolated from other people and from the flow of life, is what they dread above all else, and they will break down any barrier or taboo which makes them feel cut off from existence, regardless of the consequences or the world's opinion of them.

Because of this desire, and need, to lose their separate sense of self, and to merge with others, they can, at first, lack discrimination about people. Even chance acquaintances are seen as long-lost friends when they are feeling sociable – which they nearly always are – and one person can be almost interchangeable with another. Just so long as they are there, and ready to have fun, they will be treated like blood-brothers; until, that is, the moment passes and the party ends. Once those born under Dionysus have become clearer about what it is they really want from life, and have replaced the Cup of Pleasure with the Holy Grail as their life's goal, however, they soon learn to tell the difference between companionship and real friendship, and to understand its value. Then, chance companionship is replaced by comradeship with those who share a common vision, and their relationships take on new depth and meaning.

It is at this stage of their life's journey that they also often truly fall in love for the first time, as their close relationships follow the same pattern. Like Dionysus, who only met and fell in love with Ariadne after he had travelled the known world, they have to begin with little time, or inclination, for a serious commitment. But, when they do find the right person, they are capable of great loyalty to them, and their straightforwardness – and their ability to enjoy life, come what may – make them, in many ways, an ideal partner. Anyone involved with someone born under the Cup should not expect to get their undivided attention at all times, though, as, like Dionysus, they usually have a retinue of friends – if not a rout – in tow, and all attempts to tame them, or to tie them down are doomed to fail.

In the end, however, their real interest lies, as we have seen, in satisfying a thirst, not for fun alone, but for meaning. They are idealists at heart, with a vision of a richer, fuller life, and, when they find what they are looking for, they do not keep it to themselves, as, from first to last, they are the most companionable of people, who always want to share what they have got with others.

BORN UNDER THE CUP: D. H. Lawrence, Claudette Colbert, Jacqueline Bisset, Freddie Mercury, Lauren Bacall, B. B. King, Jelly Roll Morton, Sophia Loren, Roald Dahl, H. G. Wells.

The Cup and the Traditional Zodiac

September 11–21   The Cup and VIRGO
These Virgos are far more hedonistic and less 'virginal' and fussy than those born beneath the stars of the Great Bear. The influence of

Virgo gives detachment, and the ability to analyse experience in a cool, level-headed way to the warm-hearted, pleasure-loving Cup, and perhaps saves it from running into trouble too often.

Relationships with Other 'Lost Zodiac' Signs

The Cup with CROWN OF THE NORTH WIND
Those born beneath the Crown of the North Wind are the real soulmates of those influenced by the wine god's Cup. The Cup communicates its natural simplicity and *joie de vivre* to the complex Crown, while the Crown, in turn, helps the Cup to discover what it is they are really thirsting for.

The Cup with the RAVEN
These two constellations lie side by side amongst the stars, and they have a lot to offer one another. The Raven tends to worry about the future and the meaning of existence, and the Cup, who is an expert at trusting to the fates and enjoying the present, can help the Raven to keep balanced. The Raven, in turn, can help the Cup to look ahead and consider the outcome of his actions.

The Cup with THE SEA SERPENT
These two signs are the most sensual and easygoing. They are natural companions, but their love of pleasure and lack of discipline and boundaries can be destructive if carried too far.

THE RAVEN
Corvus

September 29–October 11

GUIDING STARS: Those born between *September 29–October 11*, beneath the glittering constellation of the Raven, are governed by **Minkar**, which marks the bird's eye, and **Algorab**, at the tip of its outstretched wing. Near the Raven's beak lie two spiralling, green galaxies, which interact with each other, known as 'the Antennae'.
PRECIOUS STONE: Jet or Black Onyx
PLANT: Comfrey (*Symphytum officinale*)

The Legends

High-flying and far-seeing birds symbolize the soul and the faculty of thought in man, and, in nearly all mythologies they are the gods' eyes and their messengers, keeping them in touch with life on earth and linking man to the divine.

While the eagle is connected with the sun and with long-range daytime vision, the raven, thanks to its black feathers, stands for the ability to see that which is, as yet, hidden and shrouded in darkness because it has not yet happened. The raven has also long been seen as a bird of ill-omen, whose appearance foreshadows doom. The Greek myth about this constellation tells us that this was not always so, however, for the raven's feathers were not always black, but silver-white, until its master, the Greek god of prophecy, Apollo, lost his temper with the bird. Apollo loved the Greek princess, Coronis, and left his snow-white raven to guard over her while she was carrying his child. But Coronis – whose name is derived from the Greek for crow, or raven – was unfaithful to the god and, despite the presence of the raven, took a mortal lover. The raven lost no time in reporting this to his master, and some say that Apollo, in his jealousy and rage, cursed the raven as the bearer of bad tidings, and turned its silvery feathers black for ever. Others claim that Apollo changed the colour of its plumage because the raven had not pecked out his rival's eyes. Either way, from that moment on, this bird which symbolized the god's prophetic powers, has been regarded as a bringer of bad tidings. This may be because, as time went on, the powers of intuition and prophecy came to be seen as the enemies of reason, rather than as true insights, and so were feared as sinister and dark, like the raven's feathers.

In the North, the Raven has also always been connected with prophetic powers. In Ireland, where the ancient gods owned ravens, they were once domesticated in order to divine the future, which they revealed, it was believed, in their cryptic croakings, while in Scandinavia they belonged to Odin, the one-eyed but all-seeing king of the gods. In order to obtain true wisdom, Odin not only hung upside-down for nine whole days and nights upon the ancient ash tree which held up the Viking universe, but also cast one of his eyes into the fountain of wisdom, in exchange for inner vision. On his shoulders dwelt Huginn and Muninn, Mind and Memory, the great ravens whom he sent out each day to question both the living and the dead, and who returned each night before dawn broke to inform him of events in this world and the next, just as Noah sent the raven from the ark in search of land. As the mind and memory of Odin, who alone amongst the gods mingled with mankind, disguised as a simple wayfarer in a wide-brimmed hat and a grey cloak, the raven stands for the ability to discover what is hidden from most eyes, and for the wisdom and true vision which can foresee the future. Like the Greek Apollo, Odin, who had stolen the mead of the poets from the frost giants, was the source not only of prophetic powers, but of poetic inspiration. Unlike Apollo, however, he was also the Lord of the other world, the leader of the Wild Hunt, riding through the stormy northern skies at midnight on Sleipnir, his eight-hoofed stallion, at the head of the Host of the Dead.

For the Native Americans, the raven is a symbol of the Great Spirit; while in the Bible it stands for God's providence, as ravens fed Elijah in the desert. It is also the heraldic bird of Denmark, and is emblazoned on the Danish standard, where, in days of yore, it was said to hang its wings if Denmark was destined for defeat, or to stand erect to prophesy a victory.

The ability to find lost property is, curiously, still known as 'Raven's Knowledge'.

The Star Sign

Intuition is the great gift of those born beneath the Raven's stars, and their ability to understand a complex situation, and, often, to foresee its outcome, however hazy it may seem to others, makes them the natural psychics of this world. As a result, they excel in any occupation which relies on the capacity to sense which way the wind is blowing, and, whether they are mediums in gipsy earrings, fashion editors, or the head of a sales force, they always have their finger on the pulse.

But intuition can be unreliable at times, and sometimes they are wrong in a prediction. As they rely so heavily on their psychic powers, this can be unsettling and disturbing for them, and, until they learn to exercise their logic and their common sense, they can, at times, feel lost and fear and worst. For, like the raven, whose feathers changed from snowy white to black, they also tend to see life in extremes. Either all is well with the world, and the future is rosy, or, if they sense some kind of problem, however minor it may really be, the skies turn black with dire possibilities and Armageddon is at hand. Usually, of course, what happens is nowhere near as bad as they have foreseen while the 'prophet of doom' mood was upon them, bu there is little anyone can do to clear away the storm clouds while the dark mood lasts. Luckily, it is not long before the sun comes out again, and, once their fears and forebodings are forgotten, they can function creatively and happily once more.

As time goes by, however, those born beneath the Raven usually learn to take their wilder, more dramatic insights with a pinch of salt. And, when they discover that almost nothing is as good or bad as they had hoped or feared, they start to find a happier balance between their intuitive and psychic side and their powers of common sense and reason, which, to begin with, they despise. Once that balance is established they really come into their own, as they can then use their extraordinary prophetic powers to real advantage. As the bird of Odin, the raven also stands for wisdom, and, once they have found their equilibrium, they, too, are able to be truly wise because, at last, they can see clearly without being blinded by their hopes and fears.

Even before they strike the happy balance, though, they can be easily distracted from their gloom by almost anything, as they are profoundly curious about life and other people, and no piece of information is too small, or trivial, to interest them. Nor does much escape their penetrating gaze. Like Mind and Memory, who kept the Norse god, Odin, well-informed about events the whole world over, they like to know exactly what is going on around them, and it is thanks to their curiosity as much as to their powerful intuition that they are able to foresee the likely outcome of events.

Their ability to delve beneath the surface of existence and discover hidden motives with what amounts to almost X-ray vision, can, at times, be disturbing to anyone involved with them, however. But they are, in fact, kindly and sympathetic people. They may see, and understand, a great deal more about you than you choose to show the world, but they are not judgemental, and they make firm and lasting friends. It is always better to have them on your side than set against you, though, as they are quite capable of broadcasting your secrets if they hold a grudge against you. If, on the other hand, you are able to cheer them up when they are low and help them to regain their sense of humour and proportion, they are unlikely to forget what you have done for them in a long while, for the Raven, which symbolizes memory, as well as insight and wisdom, does not soon forget its friends.

BORN UNDER THE RAVEN: Graham Greene, Gore Vidal, Damon Runyon, David Oistrakh, John Lennon, Verdi, Harold Pinter, Truman Capote, Mahatma Gandhi, Aleister Crowley.

The Raven and the Traditional Zodiac

September 29–October 11   The Raven and LIBRA
There are two types of Libran: one influenced by the Raven and the other by the sign of the Bear Keeper. The Raven type is far more imaginative – and less practical – than those influenced by the Keeper of the Bears, and they are also far more concerned with discovering balance, thanks to the Libran scales, which also help them to find the harmony which they are looking for.

Relationships with Other 'Lost Zodiac' Signs

The Raven with THE SWAN
These are both birds of Apollo, the god of prophecy and music, and, although they are as different as black is from white, they understand each other. The Raven can help the Swan to come to terms with life, while the Swan offers the Raven much-needed sympathy and understanding.

The Raven with OPHIUCHUS
Both these signs are concerned with understanding what makes other people tick, and diagnosing the likely cause, and outcome, of events. As a result, they work well together and they can also give mutual support in times of need.

The Raven with THE DOGS
These two are the real sleuths amongst the ancient signs, and when they get together there is almost nothing which they cannot discover. The Dogs also help the Raven to relate more fully to their instinctive side.

THE BEAR KEEPER
Boötes

October 12–26

GUIDING STARS: Two stars govern the dates *October 12–26*, **Arcturus** and **Izar**. Arcturus, the brightest star in the northern hemisphere, marks the knee of the Bear Keeper and was thought by early astrologers to bestow determination, honour and power upon those born under its influence. It is a far larger and more powerful star than Izar.

PRECIOUS STONE: Jasper

PLANTS: Plantain and Field Poppy (*Papaver rhoeas*)

The Legends

Between the Great Bear, which dominates the frozen North, and which was sacred to Artemis, the virgin goddess of the crescent moon and of wild places, and Virgo, the ancient zodiac goddess of the corn, lies one of the most mysterious figures in the heavens. His official name is Boötes – pronounced Bo-otees – the Driver of the Oxen, or the Wagon (another name for the constellation of the Plough, or the Great Bear), but he is also Arcas, the 'bear' king of Arcadia, known as the Bear Guard or the Bear Keeper.

The word 'Arcadia' still conjures up a vision of a rustic paradise, where nymphs and shepherds lived in simple bliss together in a long-lost Golden Age. There, in the mountains, shepherds, it is said, played their pipes beneath the cool shade of the spreading branches of the great Arcadian oaks, while their flocks grazed safely in the ancient woodland clearings. The people of Arcadia, the land of the great god Pan, who were shepherds, herdsmen, warriors and musicians, lived on a diet which consisted largely of acorns and believed themselves to be more ancient than the moon.

Arcas was the son of Callisto, the king's daughter. As a follower of Artemis, she had sworn a vow of chastity and spent her days hunting with her mistress through the oak-clad mountains. Zeus, the king of the gods, fell in love with her, taking on the form of Artemis to seduce her, and Arcas was conceived. Some say that Zeus, to save Callisto and her child from the vengeance of the virgin goddess, transformed her into a she-bear, and her son into a bear, and placed her in the stars as the Great Bear, with Arcas beside her to guard her. Others claim that Artemis herself turned Callisto into a bear, and that when Arcas grew up, he saw a she-bear lumbering through Zeus's temple and took aim to kill the mother he no longer recognized. Zeus, however, stayed his hand and placed them in the stars together.

Before Arcas became king, Arcadia had been called Drymodes, which means 'the land of oaks' for which this remote, mysterious area of southern mainland Greece was famous in those days. Each oak had its own spirit, a dryad or tree nymph, whose life-span matched that of her tree, and to whom offerings of wild honey, oil and milk were made. One day, as Arcas was hunting through the forests, he came upon Erato, an oak-nymph whose tree was on the verge of being swept away by a river's torrent. Arcas changed the river's course and saved Erato, whom he married.

Arcas brought momentous changes to Arcadia, the wild land that symbolizes still a lost and timeless rural Golden Age, by teaching its shepherds and its herdsmen how to grow corn, to make bread and to spin and weave. These arts, we are told, he had discovered from Triptolemus, the inventor of the wheel, as he flew through Arcadia in a chariot drawn by dragons. Triptolemus, in turn, had learned to till the soil from Demeter the goddess of the corn.

According to some legends, however, this mysterious figure in the stars is not Arcas, the son of the Great Bear, at all, but Philomelus, 'the lover of song', who was the son of Demeter, the 'law-giver' and the goddess of the harvest and the corn. Philomelus was the inventor of the wagon, for which he was immortalized amongst the stars, according to this version of the story, and from which the constellation gets its other names, the Wagoner and the Driver of the Wain. Unlike his brother, Plutus, he was content to be a humble farmer.

So the mysterious figure of Boötes, who was the son of the Great Bear, the goddess of wild virgin nature, as well as of Virgo–Demeter, the goddess of the golden corn, represents the link between civilization as we know it, and the old, nomadic cultures of the past. Lying between these two great goddesses in the stars, he is the bringer of civilization to mankind.

The move towards a settled life did not suit everyone, however. For Philomelus had a sister, Atalanta, the swiftest runner in the world – and the one who got away. Suckled at birth by a she-bear and reared by shepherds in the wild Arcadian mountains, she grew up to follow Artemis and to be a virgin huntress like Callisto.

Arcas himself can be seen as the prototype of a far more familiar figure – King Arthur – whose name means 'bear' and who has always been connected with the stars of the Great Bear, which the early English saw as Arthur's Home, or Wagon. (For more about these links with the Arthurian legends, see the myths of the Great Bear on page 67, which should also be read by anyone born under Boötes.)

The Star Sign

Those born beneath the golden star, Arcturus, have big dreams of a better, more Utopian world. But, even if their heads are sometimes in the clouds, their feet, unlike those of most visionaries, are always firmly planted on the ground, for they are extremely practical as well. They are not content until they can give their vision some kind of concrete form, and will work tirelessly, paying attention to the smallest and most boring details, to put a grand plan into action and achieve their goals.

Their ambitions are not usually for themselves, however. They are fair-minded, liberal and compassionate people, and, like Arcas, who brought agriculture and weaving to the wild land of Arcadia, they have an understanding of other people's basic needs, and a real desire to improve the lot of others. They are also highly inventive and creative, producing new solutions to old problems, and new ways to make the wheels of life run smoothly. If there is an easier way to do something, they will find it – without those born under the sign of Bear Keeper, in fact, we would probably still be living in a cave and eating roots and nuts. They do not crave luxury, but their homes are always comfortable and pretty, even when these resemble the humble dwelling of the music-loving farmer, Philomelus, rather than Camelot. They have a natural gift for transforming their surroundings and can make a home, with roses round the door, from almost nothing. They are also hospitable and good at entertaining, and usually have plenty of friends and callers knocking at their door.

They are, in short, a civilizing force in whatever sphere they find themselves, bringing order to the world around them. What they call 'delegating the work load', though, can, at times, seem bossiness, for they can become short-tempered with dreamier people born under less efficient signs, because they feel that everything depends on *them*.

They also have an eagle eye not only for the inequalities – and inefficiencies – of social life, but for its subtleties and for its funny side as well. Like Oscar Wilde, who was born under Arcturus, they are wittier and more sophisticated than most other signs, with almost X-ray vision when it comes to understanding – and exposing – the games which people play. But, even when they are impatient or sharp-tongued, they never mean to be really unkind, for deep-down they are sympathetic to their fellow mortals, and can themselves be quite vulnerable.

Efficient, civilized and witty they may be, but they also have another, more private side, and a need for peace and solitude. Without time alone – preferably as far from city life as they can get – they can begin to feel cut off from their real selves and lose their bearings. As a result, they are often happiest in relationships with people who understand this side of their nature, which often goes unnoticed, and who know how to give them the time and space to unwind and be themselves. At first, however, they often fall for people who like them for their wit and charm, but who have no real support to offer – perhaps because they do not see the vulnerable and private, hidden side. But, when they find someone who understands them, they are extremely loyal and will move mountains – or, like Arcas, change the course of rivers – to help them.

Because one part of them belongs to the city and the market-place and the other to the wilds, finding the balance between these two sides of their nature is their real challenge. And, until they do so, they can feel torn between their desire to feel that they are in the thick of things and an equally great need to be alone.

When they do strike this balance, they are able to create a unique atmosphere of peace and plenty. They are natural leaders, who understand the spirit of the times and the conditions needed for progress. They have a natural gift for mediating between people, for they are capable of great detachment and control. So much so that they can seem distant, even cold, when one-to-one relationships seem to mean less to them than the creation of some kind of Camelot. Like Arcas and King Arthur, the Bear Kings who brought about a cultural flowering in their time, it lies within the grasp of those born beneath their stars to bring about Utopia although perhaps not quite on the same scale!

However great or small their sphere of influence may be, once they have found their way in life, and discovered how to take the best from both nature and the city, and from both old and new, they can create a worthwhile and lasting set of values which enriches and transforms the world they live in.

BORN UNDER BOÖTES: Margaret Thatcher, William Penn, Dwight D. Eisenhower, Austen Chamberlain, David ben Gurion, John Wilkes, Pierre Trudeau, Lord Palmerston, Theodore Roosevelt, Karen Blixen, Captain Cook, Alfred Nobel, Christopher Wren, Anita Roddick, Pierre Larousse, Oscar Wilde.

The Bear Keeper and the Traditional Zodiac

October 12–22   The Bear Keeper and LIBRA

Both Libra and the Bear Keeper are civilized and civilizing signs, fond of beauty and order, which makes those born beneath this combination supremely able to create an atmosphere of peace and harmony around them. They also have a lighter and more subtle sense of humour than those influenced by Scorpio.

October 23–26   The Bear Keeper and SCORPIO

Scorpio is an intense and passionate sign, which motivates these Bear Keepers to carry through their dreams and plans with more determination than those influenced by Libra. They also tend to be less detached and more committed to their vision.

Relationships with Other 'Lost Zodiac' Signs

The Bear Keeper with THE GREAT BEAR

The fates of the Great Bear and the Bear Keeper are often closely intertwined, and they are always protective of each other. The Bear Keeper often helps the Great Bear to put its plans into action in a practical way, while the Great Bear, in turn, always understands and makes allowances for the Bear Keeper's need for simplicity and solitude.

∽

The Bear Keeper with THE CHARIOTEER
These are the two most practical, efficient signs and together they can reduce chaos to order in no time at all. The Charioteer, however, tends not to recognize the Bear Keeper's need for time off from the city and the market-place, and so they make better working colleagues than friends or lovers, although the Charioteer's rational approach can be most helpful to them in other ways.

The Bear Keeper with ORION
Orion, the huntsman who is happiest in wild nature and the mountains, can offer a great deal to the Bear Keeper, helping him to live his freer and more solitary side. Orion, in turn, can learn how to avoid seeing life in such an emotional way and so become more balanced.

CROWN OF THE NORTH WIND
or ARIADNE'S CROWN
Corona Borealis

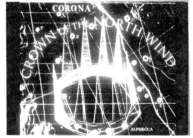

October 27–November 10

GUIDING STAR: The star which governs the lives of those born between *October 27 and November 10* is the brilliant blue-white **Alphecca**, or Gemma, the central 'gem' in the arc of seven stars which forms Ariadne's crown. It marks the knot in the ribbon along which are fastened the buds, leaves and flowers of the wreath. To the Arabs, this star was Munir, which means 'of the Babylonians', the star of those gifted in astrology. It is also said to give an active, brilliant mind and a gift for poetry and art. The constellation of Corona Borealis, which is usually translated as 'The Northern Crown' but really means 'The Crown of the North Wind', lies behind the back of Hercules: the Coronids, the meteors of the Crown, stream towards us from the direction of Alphecca during May and June.

PRECIOUS STONE: Topaz

PLANTS: Ivy, Trefoil and Rosemary

The Legends

Thirty thousand years ago in Europe, men lived in the mouths of caves and made shrines to the Great Goddess in their inmost chambers. Deep within the earth, the vast caverns of her womb-like

$\sim$
98

sanctuaries were painted with the bison and wild horses of the ancient landscape. From her all life emerged, returning to her at death, only to be born once more. The twisting, tortuous passages which led to her shrines, and which often wound for two miles in total darkness underground, were the forerunners of the Cretan labyrinth, where, 25,000 years later, Theseus killed the Minotaur with the help of Ariadne, winding to its centre on his journey of initiation, as men had done so long before.

When Theseus arrived in Crete, it was a land in need of liberation. Many years before, Minos, King of Crete had refused to sacrifice a bull sent for that purpose by Poseidon and in punishment for this broken promise the gods had inspired Pasiphaë, queen of Crete, with an unnatural passion for the great white bull; the Minotaur, Asterion, 'the starry', a human child with a bull's head, was born. To hide their shame, the king and queen asked the master craftsman and inventor, Daedalus, to create a twisting labyrinth, where the Minotaur could live in darkness, hidden from men's eyes. There he lived alone and fed on human flesh. Every seven years, seven youths and seven maidens from distant Athens were thrown to him, until one day the handsome Athenian hero, Theseus, landed on the shores of Crete, saying he was the son of the great sea-god, Poseidon. Minos threw his golden signet ring into the sea, challenging the hero to fetch it and so prove his claim. Theseus plunged beneath the waves, and swam down to the sea-nymphs' palace, escorted by a school of dolphins, and returned triumphant, not only with the ring, but with the sea-queen's wedding crown. Some say that it was made of apple blossom, and was the crown we now see in the skies. As Theseus surfaced, it dripped with water and gave off a glimmering light.

The princess Ariadne, the Minotaur's half-sister, fell in love with Theseus at first sight. The creator of the labyrinth, Daedalus, had given her a magic ball of thread, which she offered to the handsome stranger if he would marry her and take her back with him to Athens. Theseus tied the thread to the lintel of the labyrinth's door and wound his way in darkness to its centre. There he killed the lonely Minotaur with the sword which Ariadne had also given him, and retraced his steps back from the underworld into the light.

Theseus and Ariadne sailed at dawn for Athens, stopping on the island of Naxos to break their journey. There Ariadne fell asleep upon the shore and Theseus left her. Why he did so remains a mystery. When she who had been his saviour and his guide awoke alone and found him gone, she cried out to the universe for vengeance, and her voice was heard. Theseus, made careless by his triumph, forgot to lower his black sail and hoist a white one in its place, as he had promised to his aged father he would do. Aegeus, watching anxiously for his son's safe return from the high acropolis in Athens, saw the black sail and plunged headlong to his death.

Meanwhile, on Naxos the sound of laughter and of flutes and tambourines was heard, and Dionysus, the young god of wine and ecstasy, dressed in a panther skin with grapes and vine leaves in his curling hair, appeared to the weeping Ariadne, with his wild retinue of satyrs, fauns and centaurs. Soon after, they were married and Dionysus placed the crown which he had given her, made of fiery gold and red, Indian jewels set in the shape of roses, amongst the constellations.

To the old Welsh bards, Ariadne was Arianrhod, the 'silver-circled daughter of Don', the king of the fairies and the lord of the Milky Way. Her silver castle, 'at the back of the North Wind', where the souls of kings, poets, heroes and magicians went after death to await their resurrection, is the constellation of the Northern Crown, or the Crown of the North Wind, behind which lie 400 galaxies a hundred thousand light-years distant. Like Ariadne, whose name means 'the most Holy', and who is really the Great Goddess in disguise, she is the guide of the great heroes from this world to the next and back again, on their labyrinthine journey through uncharted regions of the soul to conquer death and darkness, and then to be reborn.

The Star Sign

'The child of the Crown will cultivate a garden budding with bright flowers and slopes grey with olives or green grass. He will plant pale violets, purple hyacinths, lilies, poppies which vie with bright Tyrian dyes, and the rose which blooms with the redness of blood . . . for his heart is set upon elegance, fashion, and the art of adornment, upon gracious living, and the pleasure of the hour . . .' So wrote the Roman astrologer, Manilius. With her crowns of glimmering blossoms from the sea, and red, Indian jewels set as roses, a great sense of luxury and beauty surrounds the mysterious Ariadne, princess of the colourful palace of the decadent land of Crete.

At first glance, those born under her sign often seem to be exclusively concerned with comfort, elegance and pleasure. No one has better taste or is more able to put others at their ease. But apart from their love of beauty, there is nothing simple about them, for the Crown of Ariadne, the sophisticated mistress of the labyrinth, is one of the deepest and most complex of the signs, and beneath their colourful exterior they have a much more serious side. They are a mine of information on as many subjects as you care to mention, for, like Ariadne, to whom the master craftsman and inventor, Daedalus, gave his magic ball of thread and explained the mysteries of the labyrinth, they have a great love of learning and are usually well-read. Physically, they can be quite lazy, and they often spend a lot of time curled up in a pile of cushions with a book, or discussing the meaning of existence, which they can do for hours on end. Their curiosity is boundless, for they have a burning need to understand. For them, life is a journey of discovery to find its meaning, which is hidden deep within the maze. They also seem to know instinctively that the road to the centre leads through strange realms and uncharted zones. Their real problem is that, often, they know too much, and, seeing the pros and cons of every situation, they can find it hard to make a choice and act. Words alone do not slay monsters, which is where Theseus comes in.

To those born under Ariadne, there is always something irresistible about decisive, active people like Theseus, and their arrival on the scene usually feels like a breath of fresh air, long-awaited. Here, at last, is someone who can do something about the situation. Someone who can cut a way to the heart of the matter in a few, swashbuckling strides. So Ariadne often falls in love with Theseus, putting all her know-how and wisdom at his disposal, in the hope that Theseus will free her from convoluted thoughts and make her feel alive. For Ariadne is the child of a culture which is caught up with the clever ins and outs of life, the icing on the cake, and has lost touch with freedom and simplicity in a twisting, intellectual labyrinth of its own creation.

Theseus, of course, is just as drawn to Ariadne – for a while. She is the great Initiator and Guide, the only one who knows the lay-out of the labyrinth and can help him make the journey to its centre. Theseus usually moves on, however, once he has slain the monster, looking for new challenges, leaving Ariadne weeping and alone. But only for a while.

For it is not really Theseus who is Ariadne's destined soul-mate. He may be brave and handsome, but he is also proud – and callous – and far less sensitive and wise than she is. Nor is it really Theseus who saved her from the labyrinth and the monster. Luckily for her, her wisdom does not only come from books, and her great strength is her courage – and the power of her feelings, both to suffer and enjoy. Because she loves Theseus, she acts, at last, and makes a clear-cut choice: to help him kill the Minotaur, even though the Minotaur is her brother. By doing so, she frees the life-force, whose symbol is the bull, which has lain trapped within the maze, and has become a thing of darkness only because it has been hidden from the light. Theseus may leave her, but she does not need him once the darkness has been vanquished, and when her true love, Dionysus, appears she gets her just reward and can really start to live her life.

This is, of course, where those born under Ariadne come into their own. To marry Dionysus means to learn how to let go and enjoy life, living in the moment for its own sake. The darkness of the labyrinth is replaced by sun and music. What was complicated and obscure now becomes simple, and they can start to do what they are best at, which is living for the 'pleasure of the hour', as the Romans thought they did. Offering their magic ball of thread to help others through the maze, they can guide them, too, into the light. Theseus may kill the Minotaur, but Ariadne's initiation into the mysteries of life is a journey at the end of which she learns simplicity, which is the hardest lesson, and wins the glittering crown.

BORN UNDER THE CROWN OF THE NORTH WIND:
Marie Antoinette, Ezra Pound, John Keats, Karl Baedeker, Joseph Wilson Swan (inventor of the incandescent electric lamp), Dylan Thomas, Sylvia Plath, Ivan Turgenev, William Hogarth, Fyodor Dostoevsky, Martin Luther, Louis Malle, Albert Camus, Francis Bacon, Alain Delon, John Cleese, Bram Stoker, Marina Warner (one of whose stories is called 'Ariadne After Naxos'), Catherine Tennant.

The Crown of the North Wind and the Traditional Zodiac

October 27–November 10   The Crown and SCORPIO
Scorpio is a deep and complicated sign, motivated by the need to understand the mysteries of life, and those Scorpios who are also influenced by Ariadne's Crown are the most complex of all. They do, however, have the magic ball of thread to help them to the labyrinth's heart and out again.

Relationships with Other 'Lost Zodiac' Signs

The Crown with THE CUP OF DIONYSUS
Those born beneath the Cup of Dionysus have the most affinity with those influenced by Ariadne's Crown, as they can help them to lead a happier, simpler life, as the legend relates.

The Crown with ANDROMEDA
While Ariadne's fate is to find her way through the labyrinth and out into the sun, Andromeda's is to break free from her chains. As a result, these two have a natural sympathy and understanding and Ariadne can help Andromeda to find the way. While they are both still trapped, however, they can hold each other back.

The Crown with THE EAGLE
The Eagle's clear, intellectual vision can help Ariadne through the maze, while Ariadne's understanding of the emotional realm can help the Eagle to relate better to its feelings.

The Crown with THE DOLPHIN
The Dolphin's spontaneity and love of life are sunshine and freedom to the Crown, and, in turn, the Crown can help the Dolphin to accept life's limitations.

THE SERPENT
Serpens

November 11–19 & December 24–28

GUIDING STARS: *November 11–19* Those born between these dates are ruled by the orange giant **Unuk Elhaia**, which lies 85 light-years away from us and marks the Serpent's heart.

The dates *December 24–28* are ruled by **Alya**, which is in fact two stars, not one, lying 100 light-years distant, marking the tip of the Serpent's tail.

PRECIOUS STONE: Serpentine

PLANT: Mistletoe

The Legends

The serpent, as a symbol, is probably best known to us for the legendary part it played in the downfall of Adam and Eve in Eden. It is thanks to the serpent, or so the Bible tells us, that we no longer live in paradise and that suffering and death first came into the world. But the idea of paradise, the heavenly garden cooled by crystal streams and scented breezes, and filled with shady trees and golden fruit and flowers, is far older than the Bible, and, in the earlier myths, upon which Genesis is based, both Eve and the Serpent play very different roles.

For Eve, the 'Mother of all Living', was originally the ancient Mother Goddess, and for thousands of years before the Bible, the serpent was a symbol of her power. In almost every culture, except the Hebrew one, the serpent has stood for dynamic power and life. Its ability to shed its skin made it a symbol of rebirth and immortality, while its sinuous, coiling movements, which echo the winding course of the great rivers and the life-giving subterranean waters, as well as the Milky Way, made it an image of the cosmic force which fertilizes and regenerates the universe.

About 9,000 years ago, the serpent gradually came to be seen as the consort of the goddess and not merely an expression of her power. Then, images appeared in art which show the Tree of Life, flanked by the goddess and her serpent-lover, in the timeless Garden of Immortality, beneath the crescent moon. Their union brought fertility to the earth. In this earlier garden, there is no fear of death, no punishment and no guilt or shame.

The serpent, of course, can kill, and so it also represents the goddess's power to take life as well as give it. As the Lord of Rebirth, however, the serpent itself, which can shed its skin, and which coils around the Tree of Life in many of the pictures, promises resurrection to mankind.

The ancient, bare-breasted goddess of Minoan Crete is also connected with the serpent. She holds a twisting snake in either hand, to show, perhaps, that she is queen of life and death – and resurrection. In Crete, snakes were kept as household pets and guardians of the household, and they were also known, thanks to their obvious phallic shape, as 'the husband of all women'. The spirits of the ancestors could be reincarnated as serpents and had the power, it was believed, to raise the dead, as one of the stories connected with this constellation, the Serpent, reveals.

According to this legend, Glaucus, the child of Minos, king of Crete, chased a mouse one day through his father's labyrinthine palace and disappeared quite suddenly. Asclepius, the young god of healing, led by an owl and a swarm of bees, found the boy drowned head-first in a great jar of honey in a cellar. When Minos heard, he locked Asclepius in the darkness with the body and a sword, commanding him to restore his child to life. As the eyes of the god of healing grew accustomed to the darkness, a serpent slid silently into the chamber. Asclepius raised his sword and killed it, upon which another serpent entered. Seeing its mate lying dead, it vanished, only to return carrying a magic herb, which it placed upon the head of the dead serpent, miraculously bringing it back to life. Asclepius then laid the herb – which is thought to have been mistletoe – on the drowned boy, who was also resurrected. The serpent, who had saved him, was immortalized and transformed into this constellation, which lies beside Asclepius in the skies. (See Ophiuchus on page 118 for more about the Serpent's links with healing.)

Many huge jars, each large enough to contain a human body, were discovered in the ruins of King Minos's palace. Now known as 'storage' jars, they are believed by some to have been used to mummify the dead, Egyptian-style – perhaps in honey, which was an embalming fluid – in what may have been the labyrinthine palace of dead, not living, kings and queens.

It is not only in Europe and the Near East that the serpent has been linked with rebirth and wisdom, and with the power of giving and transforming life. Una, the Australian aborigine goddess, is pictured with the Rainbow Serpent in her arms, and in India the Serpent-power, or 'kundalini', is the life-force pure and simple, lying coiled and sleeping at the base of the human spine. Through various disciplines and breathing excercises, according to the Tantric philosophers, it can be encouraged to awaken and to rise up the spine through the seven 'chakras', or body-centres, from the lowest, sexual centre to the highest, which is the third eye located in the forehead. When and if it arrives there, it is said that man achieves enlightenment and regains his lost sense of the eternal. Strangely enough, this image has much in common with the serpent coiled around the Tree of Life in the immortal garden. The tree is a symbol of the vertical axis of the world, and, like the spine, with its 'centres', linking the lowest to the highest, instinct to spirit, it also forms a link between the earth and sky. The Serpent, in both cases, promises rebirth and transformation, and not, as the Bible suggests, evil, malice and deceit.

The Star Sign

The Serpent is the subtlest and the most sophisticated of all the ancient signs, and those born beneath its stars are probably the hardest people in the world to get to know and understand, as the face they show to the world and their inner feelings are very different.

To meet, they are charm and wit personified, and, should they choose to do so, they can hold anyone spellbound for hours on end. Never boring or heavy-handed – they are far too clever for that – they can discuss most subjects with confidence and ease. And, more than other Scorpios – for most Serpents are influenced by the Scorpion of the traditional zodiac – they have the Serpent's charismatic and magnetic gaze. As a result, they are never short of admirers, but they usually prefer to keep their intimate relationships with others private. In fact, they are profoundly secretive about them, for they are very cautious people, believing that the less they give away about themselves, the stronger their position. Machiavellian intrigues and schemes are the breath of life to them, and without them they would easily grow bored, which can be a serious problem for the Serpent.

Thanks to this love of secrecy and intrigue, they have a reputation for being manipulative and cunning – which they can be – and cold-hearted – which they are not. On the surface, they may, at times, appear devious or reptilian, but if you are among the lucky few whom they eventually decide to trust and to whom they show their feelings, you will discover what loyal friends – and passionate lovers – they can be. And it is, in fact, because they are such intense, emotional people that they feel the need to exercise such caution in their dealings with the world.

The Serpent is, as we have seen, a symbol of the deeper mysteries of life. Sex, death, transformation, healing and rebirth are its domain, and the life-goals of those born under it are experience and wisdom. They are not interested in easy judgements about right and wrong. Nor in accepted codes of behaviour, which they will break without a second thought if they believe that they serve no real purpose. They may be cautious and keep a low profile, but the life-force, for which the Serpent also stands, is extremely strong in them, and they are driven by a need to discover what goes on beneath the surface of existence and to live life to the full.

They do not waste their energy on anything which bores them, though, and, like snakes, who prefer to bask quietly in the sun unless disturbed, they are not aggressive. The venom of their tongue is legendary, of course, when they are cornered, but they can also use it to expose hypocrisy and to reveal the truth, for the serpent's poison, although it can be lethal, is a symbol of healing and medicine as well. Until they learn to use this power for good, however, it is often the venom not the healing which comes through – for the life-force, in itself, is neither good nor evil. So those born beneath the Serpent who ignore the wisdom of the world and follow their own path can be quite amoral until they learn to make their own decisions about right and wrong. As the Serpent is perhaps best known for its ability to shed its skin and be 'reborn', however, those born beneath it are quite capable of doing that, and, once they have formed their own moral code, they often spend a great deal of their energy and time enlightening others.

To some, the Serpent stands for wisdom. To others, it is responsible for the Fall of Man. Either way, it is a symbol of knowledge of both good and evil, which is more important to those born beneath its stars than anything, as they believe that the truth alone can set man free. They can, as a result, appear harsh, but they are just as tough about their own illusions as they are with others. And, even then, they are never dull or earnest, because they always see – and can communicate – the funny side of life.

BORN UNDER THE SERPENT: Marlene Dietrich, Mao Tse-Tung, Mme de Pompadour, Indira Gandhi, King Louis XVIII, Eugene Ionesco, Nadia Comaneci, Ava Gardner, Humphrey Bogart, Martin Scorsese, Howard Hughes, Averell Harriman, Henry Miller, Auguste Rodin, Calvin Klein, Louis Pasteur, King Hussein, Voltaire.

The Serpent and the Traditional Zodiac

November 11–19   The Serpent and SCORPIO
Many of the traits traditionally associated with the sign of Scorpio come from the Serpent not the Scorpion. For not only the magnetic gaze – which scorpions definitely do not have – but the interest in sex, birth and death, reflect the Serpent's influence.

December 24–28   The Serpent and CAPRICORN
The influence of the Serpent adds subtlety and cunning to Capricorn's ambition, and the combination often gives great worldly success.

Relationships with Other 'Lost Zodiac' Signs

The Serpent with OPHIUCHUS
These two belong together in the heavens, and without the Serpent's depth of insight, Ophiuchus would not have such an ability to heal. Ophiuchus, in turn, brings out the Serpent's ability to be compassionate to others, and can handle him as no other sign can.

The Serpent with THE SEA SERPENT
The Serpent, who is far worldlier than his marine equivalent, can help the Sea Serpent to come to terms with living in the world, and to handle people. In return, the Serpent gains a fresher, deeper view of life.

The Serpent with PERSEUS
These two really do not trust each other although often they are thrown together and must learn to come to terms, to the benefit of both.

THE WISE CENTAUR
Centaurus

November 20–December 5

GUIDING STAR: **Alpha Centauri**, the brightest star in the constellation of Centaurus, governs the period *November 20 – December 5*. It is also known as **Toliman**, which is said to mean 'the Heretofore and Hereafter', and was believed by early astrologers to bring honour, refinement and many friends to those born under its influence.

PRECIOUS STONE: Alexandrite

PLANTS: Centaury or Cornflower

Legends

The legendary centaurs, who were half-man, half-horse, were a wild barbaric race, who lived on the mountains and wide plains of Thessaly in northern Greece, and rarely drew near to the haunts of men. The people of Thessaly were great horsemen – unusual in ancient Greece – and the sight of them on horseback, rounding up their cattle, may have given rise to the stories about these mysterious, mythic beings. Pliny, one of the great historians of Rome, however, claims to have seen one with his own eyes, which had been brought to Rome embalmed in honey.

They were immortalized in the skies as Sagittarius, the fierce archer of the traditional zodiac, but their leader, Chiron, whose sign this is, was a centaur of a far wiser and far nobler kind.

Chiron was the son of Cronus (Saturn), the ruler of the vanished Golden Age, when men lived in harmony with nature. His mother was the nymph, Philyra, whose name means both 'the lover of the music of the lyre', and the sweet-scented linden tree. Cronus took the form of a great stallion to seduce Philyra, who gave birth to her strange child in a dark cave near the summit of Pelion, a mountain thick with chestnut forests, beech trees and running streams, not far from the Thessalian plains.

Philyra, terrified by Chiron's appearance, abandoned him and he grew up alone, amongst the forest glades. He was not destined to remain alone for ever, though. Soon, he was befriended by the gods of light and reason, Apollo and Athene, who had chosen Chiron, who lived so close to wild nature, to be their pupil and the teacher of mankind. He was the first to learn medicine, science, music and the arts from them, and the greatest of the heroes were taken to him as children, to be brought up in his cave. There, he taught them all to ride, 'to shoot, to sing, to tell the truth', passing on to each of them a different branch of knowledge.

He taught Orpheus, the great musician, how to play the lyre, which he did so beautifully that animals and trees would gather round to listen, and even rivers would stop flowing at the sound.

To Asclepius, who became the god of healing, he taught medicine, for Chiron was the first physician: our word 'surgeon' (and the French 'chirurgien') comes from his name. Below Chiron's cave there lies a valley, famous for the power of its medicinal herbs, which he showed the young god how to turn into salves and potions.

To Jason, who would later sail across the seas to find the Golden Fleece, he taught the art of navigation by the stars. Even Sir Isaac Newton believed that Chiron had been the first to chart the heavens and to create the constellations. He also brought up Castor and Pollux, better known as Gemini, the Heavenly Twins of the traditional zodiac. They learned to ride from the great centaur, and joined Jason when he set off on his long quest. It was Chiron who told them all which stars to follow, but it was his daughter, Euippe, by his wife, the nymph Chariclo, it seems,

> 'Who first by oracles presages
> And by the rising stars events divined'.

(Clement of Alexandria)

She also taught physics to the young hero, Achilles, who later was to play such an important part in the great Trojan war. He had been entrusted to the centaur's care, and was brought up by him on the marrow-bones of bears and wild honeycombs, to make him strong.

At birth, Achilles' divine mother, Thetis, had tried to make her child immortal too, by submerging him in the dark, corrosive waters of the Styx, the ice-cold river which wound nine times around the Underworld. Every part of him became invulnerable, except the heel by which she held him, and it was an arrow in Achilles' heel which later caused his death. Like Achilles, Chiron was also destined to be wounded, but, in Chiron's case, the wound could not be fatal, as the centaur was immortal. The fateful – if not fatal – accident occurred at a great wedding feast beneath the spreading chestnut trees near Chiron's cave. Wine, in those distant days, it seems, was far stronger than it is today, and was normally diluted one part wine to three parts water. The wilder centaurs, whose usual beverage was fermented mares' milk, drank the strong wine neat, then went berserk and tried to rape the bride. The hero, Hercules, another of Chiron's childhood pupils, tried to stop them, and in the mayhem one of his arrows pierced the knee of Chiron, who retired in agony to his cave. Some say that, after nine days in the depths of Hades, he was transformed into a constellation and was set amongst the stars. Others claim that he cured his wound with the plant, centaury, the 'centaur's herb', and never died.

Either way, Chiron is an image of the 'wounded healer', who, because he himself has suffered, can understand – and cure – sickness and pain in others.

The Star Sign

Those born under Chiron, the wisest and noblest of the centaurs, are kind, practical, considerate people, who are naturally sensitive to the needs of others. They also have a great affinity with animals and nature. The native of Chiron, according to the Roman astrologer, Manilius, 'knows how to apply the art of healing to the limbs of animals and to relieve dumb creatures of the disorders they cannot describe for his hearing. His is indeed a calling of skill, not to wait for the cries of pain, but to recognize betimes a sick body, not yet conscious of its sickness.' Often, in fact, these people prefer the company of animals to humans, because, as Manilius says, they have a natural gift for understanding them.

Like Chiron, they can also be great scholars with wide-ranging interests, but they have no patience for dry, academic learning, which they see as dreary and one-sided. They are dextrous and like sport, and would usually rather spend their time in the fresh air, as they hate to be cooped up, and they will choose an outdoor occupation if they can. Like Chiron, who taught the heroes to ride and shoot and sing, as well as all the arts and sciences, they believe that you cannot have a healthy mind without a healthy body. Their ideal is wholeness, and even though this may not always be easy to achieve, it is what they strive towards.

No one knows better than Chiron, who was half-animal and half-divine, though, that it is hard to find the balance between intellect and instinct, mind and body. This, of course, is Chiron's wound. But without it they would be less compassionate: because they themselves have suffered, they can understand and sympathize with other people's problems. They can, and do, usually find the right balance in the end, healing the split within them, but this is something which they must work out on their own. Like all true teachers, they often find it easier to give than to receive. Because of this they can at times feel lonely and cut off, for they rarely ask for help themselves, even when they really need it, and they are at their happiest and most relaxed with people who need *them*.

They are not loners, though, and usually love family life – Chiron, after all, was happy living with his wife, Chariclo, in their cave. He has also been described as the ideal parent: for those born under his sign, the bond with children is important just as the links they have with animals and nature are strong. But they also enjoy most other forms of social life. Like Sagittarius, the other centaur in the stars, they are gregarious people, despite their love of nature and the wilds, but they do need time alone, away from city life, to recharge their batteries and unwind. The people whose company they most enjoy are often younger than themselves, and their ideal life-style consists of an extended family.

They are also, as Chiron's story shows, profoundly civilized, and although they love to give advice – even when it is not needed – they are never tyrants to their loved ones. The urge to guide and educate is so strong in them, however, that they are not usually happy until they have found a real outlet for it. But the choice of career which confronts them can bewilder them at times. Because, like Chiron, they are such all-rounders, it is not easy for them to make up their minds and settle for one thing. Anyway, they do not really like to specialize in just one field, as wholeness is their goal. If they have to sacrifice too much of either the mental or the physical side of life, they feel unbalanced and may rebel, so they need to structure their routine to make room for both. Then, their wisdom can unfold and be passed on to others, which is when they truly find contentment, for they are the great teachers and healers of mankind, and can show others how to lead a whole, and rounded life.

BORN UNDER THE WISE CENTAUR: Ian Botham, Boris Becker, Scott Joplin, William Blake, Indira Gandhi, King Charles I, the astronomer Anders Celsius, Lee Strasberg (teacher of Method acting), the astronomer Edwin Hubble, William Bonney (Billy the Kid), Jo DiMaggio, Edith Cavell, Mark Twain, Claude Lévi-Strauss.

The Wise Centaur and the Traditional Zodiac

November 20–22   The Centaur and SCORPIO
In these people the 'wounded healer' is strongly to the fore, as Scorpio also is concerned with surgery and healing.

November 23 – December 5   The Centaur and SAGITTARIUS
Amongst these 'double centaurs' are found the teachers and the scholars, as Sagittarius is the sign of philosophy, teaching and religion. They are also often more gregarious than their Scorpio counterparts.

Relationships with Other 'Lost Zodiac' Signs

The Centaur with THE LYRE
The Wise Centaur and the Lyre of Orpheus, the great musician, have a close bond, as Orpheus was one of Chiron's pupils. Music, art, and empathy with animals and nature are their common ground.

The Centaur with THE SHIP OF THE ARGONAUTS
Jason, the leader of the Argonauts, was also Chiron's pupil, and the special area shared by these two is often a love of science – and astrology.

The Centaur with OPHIUCHUS
Those born under Asclepius, the god of healing, to whom Chiron taught medicine and the properties of herbs, have, perhaps, the most in common with the noble centaur, and they are usually close and loyal friends.

The Centaur with PEGASUS
These two star signs have always been connected. Not only is Pegasus

a horse, like Chiron, but in ancient times the stars of the Winged
Horse were sometimes seen as Chiron's daughter, the inventor of
astrology.

OPHIUCHUS
The Serpent Bearer

December 6–16

GUIDING STARS: The constellations of Ophiuchus, the Serpent Bearer or the Serpent Charmer, who wrestles in the stars with the snake of medicine and rebirth, represents the Greek god of Healing, Asclepius. It is the 13th traditional Zodiac sign, between Scorpio and Sagittarius. Those born between *December 6 and 16* are governed by **Han**, **Sabik** and, at the head of the Serpent Bearer, **Ras Alhague**. Sabik was believed by ancient astrologers to give moral courage and sincerity, while Ras Alhague gave a reserved and thoughtful nature.

PRECIOUS STONE: Crystal

PLANT: Peony

The Legends

Asclepius, whose name means 'unceasingly gentle', was the Greek god of healing. Half-divine and half-human, he was the son of Apollo, the bright god of prophecy, poetry and music, and of Coronis, a mortal princess. Apollo loved Coronis, and after Asclepius had been conceived, he left a crow with snow-white plumage to guard over her, but despite its presence Coronis was unfaithful to Apollo and took a mortal lover. The crow bore the bad tidings to its master, expecting to be rewarded for its vigilance, but Apollo cursed it for failing to peck out his rival's eyes and turned its feathers black.

There are two quite different versions of what happened next. One tells us that, in his jealousy and anger, Apollo asked his sister Artemis, the goddess of the crescent moon, to kill Coronis and her lover. At the eleventh hour, however, as their bodies lay on the already burning funeral pyre, Apollo took pity on his unborn child and saved it from the flames. When King Phlegyas, Coronis's father, discovered what had happened to his beloved daughter, he gathered up an army and marched across the mountains to Apollo's famous oracle at Delphi. There, he burned the god of music's temple to the ground, for which he suffers still in Tartarus, the deepest, darkest region of the Grecian Underworld.

The people of the town of Epidaurus, the centre of the god of healing's cult, however, tell a different story. According to them, King Phlegyas and his army, accompanied by Coronis, came to Epidaurus and Coronis, who no one knew was pregnant, was delivered of her child at dead of night, in the temple of Apollo, by Artemis, the virgin huntress, and the Fates. Coronis then exposed her newborn child upon the wild slopes of Mount Titthion, still famous for the medicinal powers of the plants which grow there, but Asclepius was saved from death by a she-goat and a bitch which took turns to suckle him. When the goat-herd found them he saw the child surrounded by a bright, unearthly light, and, realizing that he was in the presence of a god, the man withdrew.

Apollo then gave Asclepius to the wise centaur, Chiron, to bring up in his cave amongst the running streams and forests of Mount Pelion, where, in the company of many other young heroes, the god of healing learned 'to shoot, to sing, to tell the truth'. More important, he learned the arts of medicine and healing from the noble centaur, who, in turn, had learned them from the gods.

Below the centaur's cave there lies a valley filled with healing herbs, whose different uses Chiron taught him, but it was not only from Chiron, and from his father, Apollo, that Asclepius, the 'unceasingly gentle', learned to heal. Athene, the grey-eyed goddess of reason also helped him by giving him two phials of the Gorgon's blood, one phial of which, taken from the right side of the snake-haired monster, whose gaze turned men to stone, destroyed life instantly. The other, taken from her left side, had the power to raise the dead. From a serpent in the Cretan labyrinth, which brought its dead mate back to life, Asclepius also learned which herb (thought to be mistletoe) conferred immortality. (See 'The Serpent' on pages 105–110.) For this reason, Asclepius's symbol is the snake, with which – as Ophiuchus – he still wrestles in the skies today.

It was Asclepius's ability to raise the dead which caused his own death, as Euippe, the first astrologer, and daughter of the wise centaur, Chiron, had once prophesied. So great were his powers over life and death that Hades, the lord of the Underworld, grew angry that the laws of fate and nature were being broken, and that his subjects were no longer in his thrall. To pacify him, Zeus killed Asclepius with a thunderbolt, and then placed him in the sky amongst the stars as the constellation of Ophiuchus.

After his death and resurrection, the cult of the young god of healing became widespread in the ancient world, and many pilgrimages were made by the sick and the mentally disturbed to his temples (which were often built near theatres), where tame serpents lived. Having been instructed and ritually purified by the priests, who made them fast and gave them bayleaves to wear and to chew, they were allowed to sleep in the inner sanctuary, or 'kline' – the 'reclining room', from which we get our word 'clinic'. The god would then appear to them in dreams, sometimes as a great serpent – a symbol of the renewal of life and energy, and of death and rebirth – or as a dog (the symbol of the instincts) or in human form, offering his worshippers cures and diagnoses.

The Star Sign

Those born beneath Ophiuchus, the Serpent Bearer in the stars, are the natural therapists and healers of the world. Like Asclepius, who was rescued from Coronis's funeral pyre, and so never knew his mother, their early life is also often unusual in some way. There are many variations on the theme, of course, but there always seems to be emotional distance of some kind – from one parent, or from both – or, perhaps, from being an only child, and so, in childhood, they can feel cut off or neglected in some way. As they are sensitive and intuitive people, this, can, at first, seem hard to handle, but it is precisely these experiences which later give them the sympathy and the compassion to put out a helping hand to others.

What they might miss as children, in their family life, is usually made up for later on in other ways, however; as they are so intuitive, and so friendly, it does not take them long to establish deep and lasting bonds with others, to which they always aspire. They also have well-developed powers of reasoning, and are unselfish, so they soon see that others have their problems too, and that everyone, to a degree, is in a similar position.

Because they tend to see life in terms of health and sickness more than other people do, they can become fanatical about their health, changing cures and dietary regimes at an alarming rate. One week's panacea for all ills is forgotten the next, when something else takes its place. No one is ever well *enough*, however rosy-cheeked and energetic they may seem, and anyone who admits to feeling under par is bombarded with a range of the latest vitamins and a great deal of advice. However well meant this may be, you often get the feeling that by turning so much of their loving care and their attention onto others, they are trying not to look too closely at themselves. This can be true, and until they do begin to listen to their inner voice and get in touch with their real feelings – which can, at times, be painful – they cannot heal themselves: and this they need to do before they can heal others.

All gifts and talents, when they remain unused and undeveloped, can turn sour and come out in surprising ways. In the case of those born beneath Ophiuchus, this often takes the form of interfering in the lives of others, and their conversation can range endlessly over a whole range of often quite imaginary woes – both their own and other people's – which they take great pleasure in discussing. Once they make contact with their real healing powers, however, and allow that energy to flow, they tend to stop just handing out advice and start listening properly. Then, they are capable of helping those who are in need of comfort to come to terms with illness and depression, and to find a new constructive way of living. Like Asclepius, who raised the dead, they seem to understand the plight of people in despair, and to know how to light a candle in their darkness, to lead them back towards a fuller, happier life.

They are, in fact extremely good at dealing with all kinds of people, as they can tune into the underlying humanity in anyone, whether they are extrovert and straightfoward, or more complex and inward-looking, like those born under the Serpent, with which Ophiuchus wrestles in the skies. This ability to get on with anyone is a rare gift, making them welcome wherever they may go, and enabling them to help others.

Because they can identify with so many different types of people, they make not only the best therapists but the best actors and entertainers, as this natural empathy means that they can enter into, and portray, almost any role. The temples of Asclepius, as we have seen, were often positioned near a theatre, to show, perhaps, that the ability to identify with a wide range of people gives both therapeutic and dramatic powers. There is another link between drama and therapy: dreams, which therapists, now as then, use to discover what is going on in someone's soul, speak to us in pictures and in stories, just as drama does, which was thought of by the Greeks as being healing to the soul. And it is, in fact, often by example, and through parables and stories, that those born under Ophiuchus manage to enlighten and to heal. There is nothing dry and academic about the way they put things over, which means that anyone, and everyone, can understand what they are saying.

They do have a tendency, at times, to identify *too* strongly with other people, though, and they can so easily absorb the pain, and the fantasies and dreams, of others that it can be hard for them to hold on to their own identity. They need to guard against this, and to learn how much of their strength they can afford to give to others, as well as where they end and someone else begins. This is especially true where intimate relationships with others are concerned, and until they learn to draw the line, they can attract people to them who take advantage of their sympathy and kindness. On the plus side, however, it is through their empathy and their ability to live out so many different roles, that they discover what it means to be a rounded human being – and the wholeness which is the aim of all forms of healing.

BORN UNDER OPHIUCHUS: Nostradamus, Robert Koch, Laurens van der Post, Kenneth Branagh, Judi Dench, John Osborne, Edna O'Brien, Edvard Munch, Margaret Mead, Rainer Maria Rilke, Frank Sinatra, Lee Remick, Roy Orbison, Noël Coward, Christina Rossetti.

Ophiuchus and the Traditional Zodiac

December 6–16   Ophiuchus and SAGITTARIUS
Although, in a sense, Ophiuchus forms a separate, 13th Zodiac sign, as it impinges on the band of traditional Zodiac constellations, it also influences those born beneath the sign of Sagittarius, and gives compassion and the urge to try to heal themselves and others to the rough and warlike centaur.

Relationships with Other 'Lost Zodiac' Signs

Ophiuchus with THE WISE CENTAUR
Those born beneath the Wise Centaur, Chiron, are Ophiuchus's guides and mentors, as they can teach them to use their gifts in a useful and creative way.

Ophiuchus with THE SERPENT
No one understands the Serpent as well as Ophiuchus, who can help these complex, private people to express themselves and find their way towards the light. Ophiuchus, in turn, can benefit a great deal from the Serpent's wisdom and its understanding of the deeper mysteries of life.

Ophiuchus with THE CHARIOTEER
The intellectual, rational Charioteer has a lot to offer to Ophiuchus, helping him to see his problems in a more detached and clearer way, while Ophiuchus, in turn, can help the Charioteer to come to terms with his emotional side.

THE LYRE OF ORPHEUS
Lyra

December 29–January 13

GUIDING STAR: **Vega,** the sapphire Harp Star in the Lyre of Orpheus, the musician, is the 'arc-light' of the heavens, rules those born between *December 29 and January 13*. It was believed to be a star of especially good omen in ancient India, because under its influence the gods had vanquished evil.

PRECIOUS STONE: Peridot or Chrysolite

PLANT: Elm

The Legends

When Orpheus sang and played the lyre, wild animals, and even trees would gather round to listen, and rivers would stop flowing, so great was the beauty of his music. Brought up by Chiron, the wise centaur (see page 112), in the wooded hills of Greece, along with several of the other ancient heroes, Orpheus went with his childhood friend and comrade, Jason, to find the Golden Fleece, and saved the ship's crew from the singing sirens with the music of his lyre.

Orpheus loved the nymph, Eurydice, but soon after they were married she died from a serpent's bite. Orpheus could not accept her death, and went down into the Underworld to play his lyre to its king and queen, hoping that they would relent and let her live once more. Even the Furies wept at the sound of his music, and Eurydice was allowed to return to the world of the living, on condition that Orpheus did not look round to see if she was following behind him. But his faith was not strong enough, and he turned – to see her fade back, for ever, into the land of shades. From then on, he could not be consoled, and was torn apart by a band of jealous women, the Maenads, when he ignored them. After his death, his head uttered oracles, and because of his descent into the Underworld, he has been compared to Christ. He was also known as the Bringer of Culture and the Father of Mysticism.

The Lyre is a symbol of the link between heaven and earth.

The Star Sign

Those born under Orpheus are romantics through and through, with their own vision of beauty and of perfection, and they are quite happy to spend hours alone in their private inner world. But they are supremely able to put into words, or art, or music, the beauty of their vision, for the Lyre is the most imaginative and creative of the signs. When they do, like Orpheus, they often strike a universal chord, which makes them fascinating to other people, for there can be something magical about them; a touch of other-worldly glamour which ensures that they will never lack friends or admirers.

Their imagination is their greatest strength and their greatest weakness, though, for the real world often fails to live up to their expectations, and they have a tendency to turn their back on life and hide behind their dreams. Because of this, they can, at times, appear aloof, and even cold. But they are not cold-hearted. It is simply that when they are bound up with what they are creating, or with some dream of happiness that lies just beyond their reach, they hardly seem to notice other people.

When they are not building castles in the air, however, they are loyal friends and lovers, with a lot of sympathy to offer, for, like Orpheus, who journeyed to the Underworld, they understand the highs and lows of love. When they fall in love, they believe it is for ever, but their idealized vision of life can make it hard for them to live in the here and now. Where love is concerned they sometimes find it easier to say goodbye than to admit that life is not a fairy tale. That would be too ordinary and boring, which is their greatest fear. Better to retain a perfect image of the beloved, all shortcomings forgotten, than to compromise it with reality. And no one will find it easy to live up to this image, at least not for a long while.

As time goes by, however, and Orpheans learn to accept life as it really is, no one has more to offer to the world than they do. They find real happiness when they can light a candle, instead of complaining of the dark, using their creative gifts to inspire others, for their salvation lies in using their potential in the real world.

The Lyre, of course, like all the signs, shows its influence in many different ways, some of which may be found on closer examination of the myth. Sometimes, those born under Orpheus have not yet found the creative artist in themselves and live life vicariously through others, seeking out creative people as their friends. Or it may be Orpheus's great affinity with nature and with animals which shows most strongly. What those born under this star all share, however, is a longing for a more beautiful and better world, and they can be found in any field where ideals can be put into practice. Politics and social work, for instance, can be the path they choose, but whichever one it is, like Orpheus, the 'Bringer of Culture', they work to make the world a better place.

BORN UNDER THE LYRE OF ORPHEUS: Elvis Presley, Pablo Casals, David Bowie, Alexander Scriabin, Francis Poulenc, Max Bruch, Sir Michael Tippett, Stephen Hawking, André Messager, Henri Matisse, Gustave Doré, J. R. R. Tolkien, Isaac Asimov, Jacques Montgolfier,

Bo Diddley, George Balanchine, Charles Edward Stuart (the Young Pretender), Augustus John, Grace Bumbry, Joan Baez.

The Lyre of Orpheus and the Traditional Zodiac

December 29 – January 13   Orpheus and CAPRICORN
Orpheus is the hidden dreamer behind the earthy sign of Capricorn, the goat which scales the mountain peaks. Often the influence of Orpheus is far more apparent than that of Capricorn in those born at this time of year, but both are ambitious, though for different things.

Relationships with Other 'Lost Zodiac' Signs

Orpheus with THE WISE CENTAUR
It is under the sign of the wise Centaur, Chiron, that those born under Orpheus find their teachers and their guides through life. For it was Chiron, who first learnt the art of music from the gods, who brought up Orpheus with the other heroes. Orpheans' affinity with nature and with animals also comes from Chiron, who was half-horse, half-man, and, just as Chiron tamed the wild part of himself, he is often there to help them do the same, and to come to terms with real life.

Orpheus with THE SHIP OF THE ARGONAUTS
Orpheus finds his friends and comrades under the sign of Jason, with whom he was brought up by Chiron. Chiron taught them both 'to shoot, to sing, to tell the truth', and they can always rely on one another. Orpheus and Gemini have a similar relationship.

Orpheus with THE SWAN:
When it comes to poetry and music, Orpheus's real soul-mate is the Swan. They share a longing for perfection, and often fall in love with each other. The Lyre and the Swan are together in the skies.

Other romantic partners for Orpheus are the Dolphin, famous for its love of music, and upon whom, traditionally Orpheans can rely; and the River of Night, who, like the rivers which stopped flowing at the sound of Orpheus's music, often fall in love with them.

THE EAGLE
Aquila

January 14–28

GUIDING STAR: Those born between *January 14 and 28* are ruled by **Altair,** the bright, pale yellow star which marks the Eagle's throat. It is said to be a mischief-maker and to give tremendous will-power and ambition.

PRECIOUS STONE: Quartz

PLANT: Eyebright (*Euphrasia officinalis*)

The Legends

The king of the birds, the Golden Eagle, is a symbol of the spirit and the sun. All-seeing, flying so fast and high, this majestic bird of prey has been sacred to the highest and most powerful gods in every land. Its elements are air and fire, and, since the earliest times, men have connected it with the thunder and the lightning which bring life and fertilizing rain to the parched earth. It stands for noble aspiration and for the highest spiritually discerning power in man.

At the funerals of the Caesars, during the great days of Rome, a captive eagle was released into the sky. It symbolized the emperor's soul, free, at last, to join the gods. Everywhere, in fact, the eagle represents the longing, and the power, of the spirit to soar upwards to the stars and to become immortal, overcoming death and bondage to mortality and earthly things. From prehistoric times, the enemy of the soaring eagle has been the serpent, which, because it creeps along the ground, has always been a symbol of the earth – and of everything the eagle wants to rise above. In Ancient Greece, the eagle was the bird of Zeus, the almighty sky-god, who lived on the cloud-capped peaks of Mount Olympus, while the serpent belonged to earth and Hera, Zeus's queen.

Legend has it that an eagle, carrying a serpent in its claws, appeared before the fall of Troy, flying high over the doomed city. The Greek priest and soothsayer, Kalchas, interpreted the strange omen for the heroes who were gathered beneath the city walls. The Trojans worshipped the Great Goddess and Earth Mother of Asia, whose symbol was the serpent. For the Greeks, however, the sky-god, Zeus, with his eagle, was the highest power. The omen therefore meant that Troy would fall and Greece would win the ten-year battle, which is in fact what happened.

Zeus and his eagle, of course, are symbolically one and same, as the most famous story about them shows. Zeus was married to his sister, Hera, but although 'her scented white arms filled the whole universe with their fragrance', he was notoriously unfaithful to her, often swooping down on unsuspecting mortal maidens, like a bird of prey. One day, however, his all-seeing eagle eye alighted on the fair youth, Ganymede, the beautiful son of the founder of Troy. Transforming himself into a great eagle, the king of the gods swept down over the broad Trojan plains, and, clasping Ganymede in his talons, soared back to Olympus. There, much to Hera's rage, the boy became the cup-bearer of the gods, who, as he filled their cups with nectar, were enchanted by his beauty. To recompense Ganymede's father for his loss, Zeus gave him two immortal mares, 'swift as the storm', and a vine of solid gold. He then turned Ganymede into Aquarius, the water bearer, and placed him in the stars beside the Eagle, where he glitters to this day. There is a much earlier belief which lies behind this story. Ganymede, it seems, was once the god, who, like Aquarius, was responsible for sprinkling the dry earth with heaven's rain. In those days, before men understood how clouds are formed, it was believed that rain came from the 'Upper Waters', the sacred source of being, over which Aquarius ruled.

In India, and elsewhere in the East, the Eagle is called Garuda, the 'fair-feathered'. He is the master of the sky who came into existence at the beginning of time, and like the Greek eagle, he is not only the enemy of the serpent, but is also connected with fire, life-giving rain and nectar. But there is an important difference. While Ganymede pours out nectar only for the gods, Garuda gives its Indian equivalent, the heavenly Soma, to all mankind. The juices of this mysterious plant are described as being 'swift as thought' – like the eagle's flight – and they give to the poet 'supernatural power, so that he feels himself immortal'. Thus, the eagle brings to human life the fiery spirit's fertilizing rain.

The eagle, though, is best known for its nobility and speed, and for the sharpness of its vision. As such, it is a symbol of the brilliance of the intellect and of insight in general. Because it flies so high, it also stands for the power of the spirit to transcend and conquer baser forces. For the American Indians, it is nothing less than the Great Spirit and represents enlightenment.

Traditionally, the eagle was supposed to be able to gaze at the sun without blinking or going blind. It was also believed to renew itself every ten years. Soaring high into the 'fiery region', it would then plunge into the sea, reappearing from the waters with new feathers and new life.

The Star Sign

Those born under Altair are usually extremely clever people. Mentally, they have twenty/twenty vision, and are endowed with greater intellectual powers than others. The lightning speed with which they grasp the meaning of a concept, or a situation, is often the envy of slower, more pragmatic signs, and, to see them in action is to watch a dazzling *tour de force*. This can make them disdainful – for being such noble creatures, they are also proud. They may ignore you – for eagles never hawk at flies – but on the other hand, they will never pick on someone weaker than themselves without good reason. They are, at heart, generous and they will choose the role of champion, rather than persecutor, of the weak. They prefer a challenge and would far rather take on someone stronger, than waste their time on those who can't compete.

However, if you have – or are – something that they want, they will swoop down, for they can be ruthless in pursuit of their ambitions. And they *are* ambitious. The Eagle's great gift – and desire – is to soar up to the highest heaven, and when they set their sights on something, they usually succeed.

When they are in a light-hearted mood, romantic conquest and intrigue also come quite high on their agenda. Like Zeus, they often have a roving eye, and the thrill of the chase gives them a great deal of pleasure. Because they know, instinctively, that confidence is attractive, they often feign indifference just before swooping down on their unsuspecting prey. But their indifference can, too easily, become genuine, once they have won the prize in what to them is often just a game.

They have a deeper and more passionate side, however. When they meet someone who lives up to their expectations, which does not happen very often, no one is more loyal. Flirtatious they may be, but they are also capable of the grandest passions, for, beneath a proud exterior, their feelings are fiery and intense, and it is often through relationships that the Eagle is transformed. For, although they may have a reputation for being fearless, Eagles are also capable of being afraid. Seeing the world so much in terms of predator and prey, of conquest and defeat, they can attribute unfriendly motives where there are none, and can become insecure or paranoid. Intellectually, they may be in a class apart, but emotionally they need as much loving care as anyone else. Asking for tea and sympathy is not their style, but they appreciate true kindness when it comes along, and are capable of great warmth and loyalty in return, for a vulnerable side softens their bold nature and makes them much more compassionate.

For all their mental brilliance, it is through their feelings that they learn about true values, and so come into their own. For the Eagle is a symbol not only of the intellect, but of the spirit, and their real goal is to overcome their baser side. When young, they can be both proud and ruthless, but, like the eagle which soars up into the 'fiery region' and then plunges deep into the sea to be reborn, they are able to transform themselves and can rise to greater heights than any other sign.

Once they have risen above the storm clouds, into the clear blue sky, they are gentler and kinder, and, because they no longer see life as a battlefield, their relationships with others become easier and more fulfilling. Then, like Garuda, the Indian eagle with his magic draught of inspiration, they can set about enlightening others, and championing the weak. They can often be found fighting for a just cause, or exposing and combating evil and oppression. No one in their right mind takes on an Eagle, while to have one on your side is, in short, to win the day.

Career-wise, Eagles excel at all pursuits which involve the use of their intelligence, their curiosity and their keen sight, like teaching or research, but, because they usually dislike routine, they are happier when they are working for themselves. Of all the signs, they make the best lawyers and detectives: just as there is nothing they cannot explain, there is also nothing they cannot find out, once they are on the trail. And Eagles do not easily give up.

BORN UNDER THE EAGLE: Joan of Arc, Martin Luther King, Edvard Shevardnadze, Benjamin Franklin, Albert Schweitzer, Thomas

'Stonewall' Jackson, General McArthur, Frederick the Great, Aristotle Onassis, Al Capone, Federico Fellini, Jackson Pollock, Sergei Eisenstein, August Strindberg, Wolfgang Amadeus Mozart, George Gordon, Lord Byron, W. Somerset Maugham, Edith Wharton, Edgar Allan Poe, Francis Bacon, Virginia Woolf, Stendhal (Marie Henri Beyle), Christian Dior and Edwin 'Buzz' Aldrin.

The Eagle and the Traditional Zodiac

January 14–21   The Eagle and CAPRICORN

These are the most ambitious, hard-working and successful Capricorns of all, as the Eagle gives breadth of vision, and an even greater sense of purpose, to the persistent, agile goat, and there is little they cannot achieve.

January 22–28   The Eagle and AQUARIUS

The Eagle and Aquarius – as Ganymede – belong together in the myths, and in the skies. Aquarius is also represented as an Eagle in the zodiac in the landscape around Glastonbury. It represents the aspect of Aquarius which can soar up into the ether and release the life-giving waters of the Urn for mankind. They are both intellectual air signs, and in those influenced by the Eagle, the Aquarian intellect is at its sharpest.

Relationships with Other 'Lost Zodiac' Signs

The Eagle with PEGASUS

The Eagle and the winged horse, Pegasus, have a lot in common, as they are both creatures of the air, but while the realm of the Eagle is the intellect, Pegasus holds sway over inspiration and imagination. When they are in accord, they make a very high-powered and creative combination.

The Eagle with PERSEUS

The Eagle and the airborne hero, Perseus, are natural friends and allies. Perseus is one of the few signs which can keep up with the Eagle, and so the Eagle does not so easily grow bored.

The Eagle with THE SERPENT
The Eagle and the Serpent often have a love/hate relationship, but they never underestimate each other, and are capable of really getting on, as the Eagle can help the Serpent to get a clearer picture of his problems, and the Serpent, in turn, can bring the Eagle down to earth.

THE DOLPHIN
Delphinus

January 29–February 8

GUIDING STARS: Usually considered as a pair, the two main stars of the sea-dark Dolphin, the pale yellow **Sualocin** and the dusky green **Rotanev**, rule those born between *January 29 and February 8*. The Dolphin, although a small constellation with no very bright stars, was believed by the ancient astrologers to have a very powerful influence over mankind.

PRECIOUS STONE: Aquamarine

PLANT: Sea Poppy or Horned Poppy (*Glaucium*)

The Legends

From the earliest times, the dolphin, the only creature on earth whose intelligence is said to be equal to our own, has been revered. A symbol of philanthropy, in Greece it was the Sacred Fish, the messenger of Poseidon, the great sea-god, and anyone who killed one wilfully was put to death.

In those days, the wine-dark Aegean sea was filled with fabulous beings, amongst whom the dolphin played. They could appear to men at any time, so it is said, and the dull blast of pink-lined conch-shell horns would herald their approach. As the wind got up, the sea-god's white horses with their fishes' tails would rise from the waters, and Poseidon's chariot, surrounded by mer-men and sea-centaurs, and by sea-nymphs and dolphins, would emerge from the spray.

Poseidon loved the sea-nymph, Amphitrite, whose name means 'the sea which encircles', but she fled from his embraces and hid herself in the furthermost part of the ocean. The sea was too large for even Poseidon to find her, so, in despair, he asked his messenger, the dolphin, to look for her and bring her back. The dolphin succeeded where the sea-god had failed, persuading Amphitrite to return with him to be Poseidon's queen in his submarine palace made of gold, deep in the Aegean. Her wedding crown, a gift from the gods, later became the crown of Ariadne, and was transferred from the sea to the stars, where it glitters near the constellation of Hercules. The sea-god was so grateful to the dolphin for his help that he immortalized him, placing him, too, amongst the stars.

Dolphins, who operate by sonar, giving off a steady stream of sounds which echo their surroundings back to them, were also sacred to Apollo, the bright god of prophecy and music. Like Apollo, they have a greater control over sound than any human musician, and are legendary for their love of music, as other stories connected with the constellation of the Dolphin show.

The musician, Arion, who was a master of the lyre, was returning by ship from Sicily to Corinth, laden down with prizes. The ship's crew turned against him, greedy for his gold, but he begged to be allowed to sing one last song before they killed him. Mounting the prow, dressed in his poet's robe, he sang a hymn to Apollo, and then cast himself into the sea, where a school of dolphins, enchanted by his music, had gathered round. He was carried to safety by one of them, who insisted on accompanying him to Corinth and the court, where, so legend has it, it succumbed to a life of luxury. Apollo, in the form of a dolphin, also saved Icadius, the Cretan, from the waves, carrying him to Delphi, Apollo's oracular shrine, to which the dolphin gave its name.

Not only to the Greeks and Romans, but to the early Christians also, the dolphin was a symbol of the saviour, the guide of souls across the sea of death. For the American Indians too, it was a messenger between the worlds. Many of the tales which tell of boys who ride on dolphins, are echoes of the ancient Greek belief that the Dolphin is the carrier of the Divine Child, the symbol of new life.

Dolphins, who spend a great deal of their time in love and play, were also sacred to the erotic goddess, Venus (or Aphrodite), and in nearly every culture, they are believed to be kinder and more sensitive than man. Unlike us, the area of their brains which has evolved furthest, controls social skills, feeling and humour; and, because sound, their main source of information, can travel through material objects, they can always sense the mood of their companions. It may well be that their powers of telepathy are also well-developed. A tribe of Aborigines, the Dolphin People of Northern Australia, claim to have been in contact with them for thousands of years, summoning the dolphins by whistling to them. When they come close to the shore, the whistling stops; then, they say, they speak with the dolphins mind to mind.

To the Maoris, the dolphin is 'Tepuhi', the sound it makes when it comes up for air.

The Star Sign

It is hard to find fault with a dolphin. That goes not only for the real dolphins, but for those born under the ancient symbol of philanthropy, the Dolphin in the stars. It is, in many ways, the perfect sign, although even those born under it have their problems, and there is always a quality about them which sets them apart.

The first thing you notice about them is how friendly and direct they are with everyone. It is always the Dolphin who picks up that someone is embarrassed or uneasy: they seem to have a sixth sense which tells them instantly how other people feel. With their humour and playfulness – and their sympathy – they are able to make those around them unwind and relax, and they never use their almost telepathic powers to take advantage of others. Dolphins are not manipulative people, and they have no time for those who are – a characteristic they can divine, however well it is disguised. When they are young, however, and inexperienced, they can find other people's motives hard to comprehend, and, even when they have learned more about the world, they can, at times, be too naïve and trusting.

Their lack of aggression can belie their strength, which is in fact tremendous. When roused to anger, like their namesakes who can dispatch a shark far larger than themselves, they will move in like greased lightning for the kill – but only if the opponent refuses to back down, and really seems to want to fight. Even when they are angry, they are fair, and will avoid a confrontation if they can find another way of dealing with a tricky situation. Dolphins are far more interested in love than war, and love, romance, and flirtation, take up a great deal of their time. Sensuous and erotic, as their connection with the voluptuous goddess, Venus, shows, they can appear amoral to more inhibited and straitlaced people, but, in fact, their passionate pursuit of pleasure and their love of fun are always innocent and spontaneous. They are puzzled by the puritanical disapproval which comes their way, as, even if they find it hard to be monogamous, they are never knowingly unkind to friends or lovers.

They are naturally outgoing and gregarious, and, on the whole, do not like to be alone. They make kind and loving parents, according to the early astrologers, and loyal, considerate friends, but they would rather live in an extended group of people than in a closed one-to-one relationship. They need friendship and feel deprived without it. Nor, if they can help it, will they stick at one thing for long; but even if they spend less time working and more time playing than other signs, their natural intelligence and curiosity usually get them just as far in life as those who work from nine to five. They are creative, and, like most creative people, they prefer to work in fits and starts, but, when the spirit takes them, and their heart is in it – which is usually the case with art or music – they can achieve the goals they set themselves with ease. They are quick learners and can effortlessly master any subject if they try, but a regular routine and steady job cramps the freedom without which they do not feel alive. Like the dolphins, they would rather live simply and be free, even if that means cutting down on material possessions. If money does fall into their lap, however, they will use it and enjoy it to the full.

Apart from their great aptitude for music – and for having fun – the Dolphin's greatest gift is helping others, and, like the dolphins who rescued shipwrecked sailors, they excel at, and enjoy, playing the role of guide and saviour to both friends and strangers. The Dolphins' unerring instinct for the feelings of others makes them particularly kind and sensitive. It seems that, like the dolphins who have recently befriended swimmers, they are often able to buoy up others just by their presence. The ancient Greeks, as we have seen, worshipped the dolphin as the carrier of the Divine Child, the symbol of new life, and their high spirits, their straightforward generosity and their desire to help, can, it seems, bring new life and hope to those who really need them.

But, being so telepathic that they soak up the atmosphere around them, can cut both ways. They can quite easily be overwhelmed by other people's moods and find it hard to distinguish between these and their own. When they feel threatened in this way, or if society attempts to tie them down, their natural instinct is to run. Normally so easy to get on with, they can then be very stubborn, for they cannot bear to be subject to restrictions – and this can make it hard for them to come to terms with life in the real world. This independence of spirit is their greatest fault – if it can be called a fault, given that, although they are determined to live life according to a private moral code, they are always kind, and their manners are always of the heart.

BORN UNDER THE DOLPHIN: Norman Mailer, Nell Gwyn, William Burroughs, Jules Verne, James Joyce, Boris Yeltsin, Vanessa Redgrave, Felix Mendelssohn-Bartholdy, Frederick Delius, Franz Schubert, Anton Chekhov, Charles Dickens, Sir Francis Pettit-Smith (inventor of the screw-propelled ship), James Dean, Anna Pavlova, Germaine Greer, W. C. Fields, Lana Turner, Zsa Zsa Gabor, Bob Marley, Freya Stark.

The Dolphin and the Traditional Zodiac

Janaury 29 – February 8   The Dolphin and AQUARIUS
Aquarius is famous for its abstract love of humankind, and in those born under the combined influence of these signs, the spirit of philanthropy is strong. These are the most unconventional, warmhearted and easygoing Aquarians, with the greatest need for freedom.

Relationships with Other 'Lost Zodiac' Signs

The Dolphin with THE EAGLE
The Dolphin is the messenger of the sea-god, Poseidon, and the Eagle that of the sky-god, Zeus. The Dolphin is as fast and sure in the emotional and intuitive element of water as the Eagle is in the air, the element of intellect and abstract thinking. This gives them a strong bond, as, although they are so different, they need each other to achieve a balance.

The Dolphin with CROWN OF THE NORTH WIND
It is the dolphins who help Theseus to find the sea-queen's glimmering crown – later transformed into the Crown of Ariadne – in her palace deep beneath the waves. In Ariadne's quest for simplicity, it is often the Dolphin, so straightforward and so free, who can help her to escape from the darkness and complexity of the labyrinth.

The Dolphin with THE SEA SERPENT
The Dolphin and the Sea Serpent are soul brothers – or sisters. They

are both creatures of the watery deeps, and understand each other without recourse to words.

The Dolphin also has a great affinity with other watery signs: The River, the Swan, and the Ship.

THE SWAN
Cygnus

February 9–29

GUIDING STARS: Those born between *February 9 and 13* are governed by **Sadir**, at the Swan's heart, seen as the most quick-witted and mercurial of its stars. The star for *February 14–19* is the warlike **Gienah**, on the outstretched wing; and for *February 20–29*, the Venusian **Deneb**, the brightest star on the Swan's body, which makes those who come under its influence dreamy, cultured, contemplative and adaptable.

PRECIOUS STONE: Moss Agate

PLANTS: Poplar and Narcissus

The Legends

'In its own person, the Swan hides a god and the voice belonging to it; it is more than a bird and mutters to itself within.' So wrote the Roman astrologer, Manilius, about the swan, which, as legend has it, sings ecstatically before it dies. The belief that there is something both supernatural and human about this noble bird appears to be almost universal. Swans as mysterious, other worldly maidens, or as gods who can change shape at will – or as human beings who have been cursed and transformed, abound in myth and folklore.

To the Greeks, the constellation of the Swan was identified with Cycnus (or Cygnus), the friend and lover of Phaethon, in whose hands the horses of the sun-god's chariot careered out of control. When Phaethon plunged headlong to his death into the waters of the river Eridanus far below, Cycnus came to search for him, and, as he gazed mournfully into the river's depths, was transformed into a swan. Phaethon and Cycnus share another link, in that it was the Swan which pulled the Sun's barque over the waters of the night, handing over, as dawn broke, to the horse-drawn sun-chariot which Phaethon drove. The same idea is found in Finnish myth, where the Swan floats on the river of the Underworld, Tuenola, singing the Song of the Dead.

The Swan has many links with music and with death and is a symbol of the mystic journey to the other world. Apollo, the Greek god of light, poetry and music, rode in a chariot drawn by swans, and was believed to have turned into one. The souls of all great poets were thought, at death, to be similarly transformed, while the souls of kings were transported on their backs to the paradise at the Back of the North Wind – a belief which comes, perhaps, from the haunting sound they make as they fly north in summer to their Arctic breeding grounds. For the Celts, however, their melancholy call was said to be the voice of the Children of Lir, the sea-god, who was the origin of King Lear. Cursed and transformed into swans by their wicked stepmother, they were condemned to fly, until the dawn of Christianity, across the lonely lakes and streams of Ireland.

The same theme of bewitchment and redemption is found in fairy tales and in the mysterious story of the Swan Knight, Lohengrin. Appearing in Antwerp as the champion of the princess Elsa, in a skiff drawn by a swan, Lohengrin saves Elsa from the schemes of the evil sorceress, Ortrud. Lohengrin and Elsa marry, but on the sole condition that she does not ask his name. On the wedding night, however, Elsa asks the fatal question and Lohengrin, under oath to answer, reveals his name. As he does so, the swan returns for him, and Lohengrin transforms it in Elsa's long-lost brother, who had been bewitched by the sorceress, Ortrud. Elsa thus regains her brother, but loses Lohengrin, who disappears.

Lohengrin, it seems, is the male version of the more numerous Swan Maidens of northern lore. The warlike Valkyries, for instance, who appeared over the blood-stained Viking battlefields, carrying off the dead to an eternal banquet in the skies, could turn themselves into swans at will. In Celtic myth they are less fierce. There, they were often caught by men who stole their magic feathered 'swan-shifts', and, held in thrall, were forced to live in human form until a knight appeared to save them, or their captor asked them a forbidden question. Even when they seemed completely human, though, their true nature was revealed by the gold or silver chain they always wore. Swans were also thought by some to take on human form when they flew north together in the Summer.

Nobler and more powerful than the mysterious trapped beings in their swan-shifts, however, was the swan maiden, Ibormeith. As Angus, the beautiful young Irish god of youth and love, lay sleeping, she appeared to him in a dream. When he awoke and found her gone, the young god grew sick with love and longing, but eventually he found her on the shores of Loch Bel Dracon on the ancient Celtic feast of Samhain, or Hallowe'en. Ibormeith, who spent alternate years in swan and human form, had one hundred and forty-nine other swan maidens for companions. When Angus found them by the water's side, he turned himself into a swan and they flew together, singing, three times round the lake. So beautiful and magical was the music of the swans that all who heard it fell asleep for three whole days and nights. Angus then returned with Ibormeith to his home, Bruigh na Boinne, or New Grange, the 6,000-year-old megalithic mound on the banks of the River Boyne in County Meath.

The swan, which is at home on land as well as in the air and water, and has, perhaps, therefore been seen as a beautiful, mysterious being which hovers between the animal, the human and the divine, is a symbol for both transformation and redemption.

The Star Sign

The noble swan, with its long, arching neck and curving wings, is the most graceful of all birds, and grace – of both body and spirit – is a quality which those born beneath its brilliant summer stars have in plenty. Often, they are also blessed with striking looks, though they do not pay much attention to how others see them, for, flying high above the mundane world, they often seem to be bound up with their own thoughts and dreams. Whatever work they do, they are, at heart, poets and musicians with a great love of beauty – and they are often psychic too. Like the swan, which spends so much of its time gazing down into the river, they are deep, contemplative, unhurried people who are much more interested in what lies beneath the surface of existence than they are in superficial things.

They are extremely adaptable, however, and they can – and will – play almost any role that is required of them, for they are always eager to please. Sometimes too much so, and, like the Ugly Duckling who did not know it was a swan, and wanted to fit in, they often feel uncertain about who they really are and what they should be doing. Discovering their true selves is the real life-journey of those born beneath the Swan, which not only looks into the depths, but also seems to gaze curiously at its own reflection as it floats across the waters. But they should beware of becoming too self-absorbed.

Because they are adaptable – or innocent – it can be easy for others to take advantage of them, forcing them into ways of life which do not suit them and which do not allow them to express themselves. It is not so easy to tie them down, though: just when they seem most passive and willing to oblige, they have a knack of disappearing, like Lohengrin, or the mysterious swan-maidens who could transform themselves and vanish without warning. Even when they play the required role, and harmony and peace seem to prevail, there is often a private part of their nature which they keep hidden and which remains untamed. When pushed too far, they will defend their own with surprising ferocity and force. The temptation for them to escape into their dreams can be great, for their dream world is a rich one and – not surprisingly – they prefer the quest for eternal truth and beauty to the tedium of everyday routine.

Unfortunately, as long as they continue to fly off into their dreams, they do not feel at ease or whole and centred, nor do they receive the response and respect which they deserve. When someone comes along, however, who understands their complex nature and wants to help rather than control them, their wild, swan nature can be humanized and integrated into their daily lives. But it can take time – and patience – for them to trust someone enough to allow them really close.

Success comes when the Ugly Duckling knows that it really *is* a Swan, and learns to use its insight and its vision in this world, instead of taking off into the blue. When Swans manage to achieve this, and so become whole, they probably have more to offer in the way of truth and beauty than almost any other sign – except, perhaps, those born under the Lyre of Orpheus, the musician, which lies close by in the stars, with whom they have a lot in common. Even when they do become more rounded, balanced people, and grow into themselves, there is always something mysterious about them, as though they were not quite prepared to be as others, or did not quite know how. For the Swan, after all, does not spend a great deal of its life on solid ground; it is a creature of the skies and of the waters, and, ultimately, its great gift is the ability to see into the heights and depths, and to communicate its vision, as well as to transform itself.

BORN UNDER THE SWAN: W. H. Auden, Stephen Spender, Brendan Behan, Victor Hugo, Henry Wadsworth Longfellow, Boris Pasternak, George Frideric Handel, Gioacchino Rossini, Enrico Caruso, Nina Simone, Marie Rambert, Andrés Segovia, Harold Arlen, Sir Geraint Evans, Sir Vivian Fuchs, Sir Ernest Shackleton, Charles Darwin, Barry Humphries, Frédéric Chopin.

The Swan and the Traditional Zodiac

February 2–18   The Swan and AQUARIUS

Aquarius is an idealistic, but intellectual sign, which gives detachment and the ability to analyse emotions to the intuitive, poetic Swan. This is a good combination, although it can be quite escapist.

February 19–29   The Swan and PISCES

The tendency of these Swans to daydream is even more pronounced than it is in those born under Aquarius, but it is a truly gentle and poetic combination.

Relationships with Other 'Lost Zodiac' Signs

The Swan with THE RIVER OF NIGHT

This is a real love-match as these two signs understand each other and never tire of each other's company, as they have a lot to learn from each other.

The Swan with ANDROMEDA

These two signs share a desire for freedom, and are deeply sympathetic to each other, although at times they can make each other more defeatist.

The Swan with THE LYRE OF ORPHEUS

The Swan and the Lyre, which are together in the heavens, share a love of music, and of beauty of all kinds. They also understand each other as they are both dreamers and idealists, which gives them a strong bond. They can, however, encourage each other to be unrealistic about life.

The Swan with THE DRAGON

These airborne beings are very different from one another but can balance one another well. The Swan softens the Dragon's fire and anger, and is sympathetic to its vulnerable side, while the Dragon gives the Swan drive and determination.